GOD'S WELCOME

A Co-Creative Vision of the Spiritual Exercises
of St. Ignatius for Women

by

CYNTHIA BYERS WALTER

DORRANCE
PUBLISHING CO
EST. 1920
PITTSBURGH, PENNSYLVANIA 15238

Dorrance Publishing Co
585 Alpha Drive
Suite 103
Pittsburgh, PA 15238
Visit our website at *www.dorrancebookstore.com*

ISBN: 979-8-8860-4140-8
eISBN: 979-8-8860-4805-6

GOD'S WELCOME

**A Co-Creative Vision of the Spiritual Exercises
of St. Ignatius for Women**

by

CYNTHIA BYERS WALTER

Dedicated to those
who welcome others
in the name of God.

CONTENTS

ACKNOWLEDGMENTS

I am indebted to Sister Carole Riley, CDP, PhD, who not only believed that this book needed to be written, but also somehow believed that I was the one to write it. I give heartfelt thanks to the welcoming and courageous women who "test drove" this book at Emmanuel Episcopal Church in Harrisonburg, Virginia, and St. Paul's Church in Mt. Lebanon, Pennsylvania: Jane Adams, Lyn Babcock, Dee Childs, Lois Cusack, Jill Gordon, Maggie Kyger, Annette Paxton, Kathryn Powell, the Rev. Claudia Seiter, Eileen Sharbaugh, and Carol Warner. I thank the Rev. Ted Babcock for inviting me into the vibrant and prolific Ignatian ministry at St. Paul's. My fondest thanks go to my number-one fan for 40 very odd years, Rich Walter. Mostly, I thank God for all of you. To God be the glory.

INTRODUCTION

WELCOME

The welcome mat is out. The door is flung open. Someone waits within with arms outstretched to receive you. You rush forward with absolute trust into a loving embrace. Comfort, safety, sustenance, and nourishing conversation await. God's welcome gives way to freedom, transformation, vocation, and abundant life.

You may have picked up this book because you already know something of God's welcome; or your experience of God may not be nearly as welcoming as the preceding paragraph describes. Whether or not you have experienced God's welcome will depend on your past relationships with other people and with the church. Some of us have been warmly embraced by church, some of us have not, and some of us have been conditionally embraced or initially embraced but relegated to circumscribed roles.

Unlike humans and human institutions, God loves unconditionally. Learning to trust that love is key to accepting God's welcome. The more we trust the welcome, the more we know the freedom and transformation that God promises us.

To be sure, Christian tradition has presented God as authoritarian and judgmental at times. Much of the Bible itself reflects what Nan C.

Merrill calls "a patriarchal society based on fear and guilt."[1] An undue emphasis on scriptural passages about sin and judgment obscures both the embracing love of Jesus and the invitation to co-creation which has been part of God's relationship with humanity from the beginning.

In my capacity as a spiritual director, I have found the same thing to be true with the Spiritual Exercises of St. Ignatius. It is understandably easy for a book intended to provide direction to come across as a rulebook rather than a guide to the deepening of a lifelong, life-giving relationship. However, the rulebook approach undermines the incomparable value of the exercises to transform lives, suppressing God's welcome.

Katherine Dyckman, Mary Garvin, and Elizabeth Liebert have researched extensively how the language so far used in treatments of the Spiritual Exercises has failed to resonate with women's experience in particular. Their book, *The Spiritual Exercises Reclaimed: Uncovering Liberating Possibilities for Women*,[2] directly inspired the book you hold in your hands.

Though I conceived this book as an adaptation of the Spiritual Exercises specifically for women, I discovered that there are others who have experienced the same issues as women often do with what is perceived as the judgmental terminology and authoritarian tone of the exercises. What I have concluded is that altogether too few people experience God as welcoming.

In adapting the Psalms for modern devotional purposes in her *Psalms for Praying*, Merrill focuses on the "reciprocity of Divine Love," going on to observe in the preface to her book that, "Affirming the life-giving fruits of love and acknowledging the isolation and loneliness of those separated

---

[1] Nan C. Merrill, *Psalms for Praying: An Invitation to Wholeness* (New York: Continuum, 2007), ix.

[2] Katherine Dyckman, Mary Garvin and Elizabeth Liebert, *The Spiritual Exercises Reclaimed: Uncovering Liberating Possibilities for Women* (New York: Paulist, 2001).

from Love, may serve to awaken the heart to move toward wholeness and holiness."[3] My hope is that *God's Welcome* presents the exercises in the same spirit Merrill describes for her psalms: "a spirit of cooperation, co-creation and companionship with the Beloved."[4]

My own concept of "co-creation" is based on three points of theology. First, God created human beings in God's image. One implication of this doctrine is that we are creative as God is creative. Though our creativity is limited, insofar as we are creative we reflect God's likeness. Secondly, God calls us into relationship with Godself. Though part of that relationship involves our simple adoration of God, God also welcomes conversation with God's people. Thirdly, God calls human beings to participate in God's great work of redeeming the world. That is what the kingdom of God is all about. Our call to co-creativity with God invites a dialogical approach both to the Bible and to the expression of our own spirituality.

While attempting to remain true to the original Exercises, I have tried to present them in a more dialogical format that respects the range of experience of women and others from a non-dominant culture. I wish to welcome both the gifts and the sorrows of those who have felt "separated from Love" for whatever reason. My vision is to approach the Spiritual Exercises in a spirit of co-creation and cooperation, that God's welcome may be known.

~ ~ ~

The balance of this introduction supplies background information intended to support your discernment about whether this program is for you. Bear

---

[3] Merrill, *Psalms for Praying*, ix.

[4] Merrill, *Psalms for Praying*, x.

in mind, however, that the rest of the book will not be so didactic. The exercises that follow invite you to invest yourself profoundly in a journey with Jesus through dialogue with God, guided by the Holy Bible, and illuminated by the holy scripture of your own heart.

LIFE OF ST. IGNATIUS LOYOLA

For those unfamiliar with Ignatian practice, we will begin by meeting its founder.

Ignatius was born in 1491 in Basque country, the mountainous region between Spain and France. Of noble blood, he sought to emulate the swashbuckling knights of legendary fame and distinguish himself in battle. In 1521, a cannonball shattered both his right leg and his dreams of being a famous soldier. During a long convalescence, he found himself dissatisfied with the chivalric romances that once fired his imagination and, asking for other reading material, was given religious tracts on the lives of Christ and the saints. Here he found peace and consolation. He experienced a deep conversion and realized that his future was as a soldier for Christ.

Ignatius developed a strong spirituality and wrote in his notebook about his experiences. When he shared these writings with others, many responded to his practical and sensitive approach to seeking and serving Christ in the world. His instructions to them evolved into the Spiritual Exercises, which have guided spiritual seekers ever since.

Eventually ordained a priest, Ignatius realized he did not have a monastic vocation. He continued to live in the world, taking vows of poverty and service to the poor. His vowed followers became known as the Society of Jesus, or the Jesuits. Many laypersons also accepted Ignatian practice and discipline.

Ignatius had run-ins with the Inquisition even after the Vatican had formally recognized the Society, but his influence was, and continues to be, formidable. Ignatius died in 1556 and was canonized by the Roman Catholic Church in 1622. The Spiritual Exercises are his best-known work

THE SPIRITUAL EXERCISES AND THE NINETEENTH ANNOTATION

Intended as instruction for the spiritual director, The Spiritual Exercises consist of 370 paragraphs, numbered to allow for easy reference. For example, "SE 165" refers to the paragraph describing "the first kind of humility." Note the "SE" prefix, which is standard no matter what translation or edition you use.

In SE 18, 19, and 20, Ignatius lays out three distinct ways in which the director can guide the one "making" the exercises. SE 18, or the Eighteenth Annotation, allows the spiritual director to give a few select exercises to those who have specific spiritual needs and limited time, adapting to the individual's aptitude and interests.

SE 20, or the Twentieth Annotation, describes the classic 30-day retreat, in which the person making the exercises removes herself from her daily routine to work through all the exercises in an intensive format, typically in a retreat center or monastery. For Ignatius, the virtue of the Twentieth Annotation is that the mind, relieved it of its engagement in "many things," can devote its full attention "to one single interest...the service of its Creator and its spiritual progress" (SE 20).[5] Persons discerning a call to ordination or the religious life often choose this form of the program.

Like many people, you may find it difficult or impossible to shed your everyday responsibilities for 30 days. If so, you are part of the target

---

[5] Ignatius of Loyola, *The Spiritual Exercises of St. Ignatius: Based on Studies in the Language of the Autograph*, translated by Louis J. Puhl, S.J. (New York: Vintage, 2000), 11.

audience for whom Ignatius developed the Nineteenth Annotation, the subject of this book. The Nineteenth Annotation covers the same ground as the Twentieth Annotation, but it does so over a period of about nine months. In this way, you can keep up with household and work obligations while applying your new learnings and insights to your daily life.

THE FOUR WEEKS

The complete Spiritual Exercises, whether in Nineteenth or Twentieth Annotation format, are divided into four "weeks," framed by the First Principle and Foundation at the beginning, and the Contemplation to Attain Love at the end. The "First Week" supplies meditations on the foundation of God's love and how human beings betray it through sin. The "Second Week" journeys with Jesus throughout his earthly life. Christ's Passion and Death occupy the "Third Week," while the "Fourth Week" emerges into the glories of Jesus' Resurrection and Ascension.

During a 30-day retreat, Ignatius' "weeks" may or may not correspond to seven-day calendar weeks. For the one making a Nineteenth Annotation retreat, each Ignatian "week" may occupy several calendar weeks. This can create confusion. For the purposes of this book, I will use quotation marks when referring to one of the four Ignatian "weeks."

THE SPIRITUAL DIRECTOR

Ignatius designed all versions of the exercises to be worked under the supervision of an experienced spiritual director. Self-directing the Nineteenth Annotation is not recommended. Making the exercises tends to release strong spiritual forces. In Ignatius' own words, "commonly the enemy of our human nature tempts more under the appearance of good when he is exercising himself in the illuminative way" (SE 10).[6]

A trained director recognizes signs of God at work in the person's life, and the signs of ungodly forces as well. The director supplies valuable encouragement, correction, guidance, and accountability.

Before beginning the exercises in this book, or in any other form, you will therefore want to find a spiritual director, preferably one trained in the Nineteenth Annotation. Your pastor may be able to advise you. A nearby convent, monastery, or retreat center would be another resource. You may also consult Spiritual Directors International,[7] which maintains a list of directors, their locations, and specialties. Many directors are now able to meet virtually, so physical distance between you and your director need not be a barrier.

COMMITMENT

Undertaking the Nineteenth Annotation is a serious commitment. If you are considering the exercises, dedicate some time beforehand to discern whether you are being called to undertake them. To complete the exercises using the Nineteenth Annotation takes several months. It seems more than a coincidence that the exercises have approximately the same duration as human gestation, and for the same reason: the formation of new life takes time.

---

[6] Ignatius, *Exercises*, 7.

[7] "Find a Spiritual Director/ Companion Guide." Spiritual Directors International, last modified 2021, https://www.sdicompanions.org/find-a-spiritual-director-companion/ (downloaded 8/11/2021).

YOUR DAILY PRAYER TIME

The person making the exercises typically allows for at least 45 minutes of dedicated prayer each day. If that seems daunting, consider that 45 minutes a day is not excessive for practicing a musical instrument or daily physical exercise. Dedicated prayer is a discipline like any other. A person makes time for things that are important.

At first it may be difficult for you to dedicate 45 minutes to prayer. Be gentle with yourself. Start modestly and work your way up. If you *schedule* the 45 minutes, however, even if you don't fill every second with prayer, you will have broken the busy-ness cycle, which will allow you to listen to your heart. You may find you can sit still for longer than you thought.

You will probably want to combine different forms of prayer in your daily prayer time. Your prayer time may include not only the Bible reading and reflection suggested in the exercises that follow, but also a period of centering prayer, journaling, music, yoga, or artwork. If you are already profitably practicing some form of daily prayer, incorporate that into your Ignatian prayer time.

The next chapter provides exercises in different forms of prayer.

THE EXAMEN

The examen, also known as the General Examination of Conscience, distinguishes Ignatian spirituality. Practicing a daily examen is as integral to the Nineteenth Annotation as the daily reading and praying exercises.

Ignatius recommends doing the examen twice a day, once in the afternoon and again before bed, but the most important thing in undertaking this discipline is to do it at least daily. Many will find one bedtime examen most natural. Others will do the examen upon rising, reflecting on the previous day. The best way to do the examen is in a way that most easily becomes habitual for you.

Think of the examen as a conversation between a loving parent and a cherished child. After a prelude of self-situating physically, mentally, and spiritually in the loving presence of God, the classic Ignatian examen consists of five steps: gratitude, petition for an honest and fruitful examen, review of the last day, forgiveness (where needed), and renewal.

The next chapter will discuss the examen in greater detail.

READING THE BIBLE

Nearly all the exercises involve meditation on a Bible reference. For the purposes of these exercises, I encourage you to engage the Bible dialogically. This means being less concerned about the one unchangeable truth in each passage than about what God may trying to communicate to you personally at this specific point in your life and prayer.

The Bible is a living document. It is a conduit of communication between God and God's people. In any given passage, God may have something to communicate to you personally at this particular time that someone else may not "hear." There may even be something that you might not hear yourself if you read the same passage under different circumstances. That is why we read the Bible again and again.

Some of the excerpts suggested in these exercises are very brief. Feel free to read a longer selection if you are so moved.

Some passages may strike you negatively. This can be a very good thing if from it you learn something about yourself and your relationship with God. Use the opportunity to open a conversation with God. Journal about it. Discuss it with your director. Know that whatever feelings the exercises arouse in you can help you grow.

The use of commentaries is not necessary. If you use a commentary, please do so sparingly. The emphasis in the exercises is transformation of the soul, not intellectual comprehension.

The next chapter offers an exercise on reading the Bible dialogically according to a time-honored method called *Lectio Divina*.

JOURNALING

Though journaling comes naturally to some, others find it challenging. Yet a journal is an invaluable aid to becoming aware of interior movement. Cultivating this awareness is essential in an Ignatian retreat, whether in the classic 30-day format, or, using the Nineteenth Annotation, doing the exercises over a period of months. If you are beginning the Nineteenth Annotation, this is the time to begin to keep a journal if you are not keeping one already. If in the past you have tried to keep a journal and given it up, try it again using the following suggestions.

First, choose a format you are likely to stick with: either handwritten or typed on a keyboard. Personally, I find using non-technical tools more supportive of spiritual activity, but do what feels right for you.

With a handwritten format, you can use a spiral notebook left over from college, but for many it is helpful to buy a blank, bound journal from a bookstore. This is holy business, and dedicated, handsome furnishings, appropriate to the dignity of what you are about, are as important as they are in church. You may also wish to choose a special writing instrument.

To get you started, a journaling exercise follows at the end of this introduction. Consider it a "warm-up."

HOW TO USE THIS BOOK

This book provides meditations for every day of the week, each week building on those preceding. For this reason, it is best to take them in order and not to skip ahead.

Each chapter begins with some contextual material that introduces the theme for the next several weeks. Each week names a "grace" to be explored in the exercises that follow. Pray for the grace of the week each day. This practice will supply shape and direction for your meditations.

The questions provided are intended to guide and deepen reflection and encourage dialogue with the material. Do not feel you have to answer every question as if you were taking a written exam. If your heart leads you in a different direction, follow it. Just be sure to follow your heart's promptings and not just intellectual curiosity.

As I have written this book, I have prayed earnestly for you who will be making these exercises. Through them, may you be richly blessed with a closer, deeper, transformative relationship with the One who made you, cherishes you, and welcomes you.

JOURNALING EXERCISE

Open your journal to a fresh page. Staring at a blank page is the surest way to inspire writer's block, so write something, anything. The easiest thing to begin with is the day's date and the day of the week. If the day is special to you (like a birthday or anniversary), add that. If it is a Sunday (like "Pentecost 3") or Holy Day and this kind of thing is important to you, write that next. The important thing is to get something on the page.

Here it becomes personal. If you do not know where to start, you might take a self-inventory. Begin by registering any interior sensation, like aches and soreness, growly tummy, breathing, or heartbeat. Next, consciously review what your senses are telling you right now: what you see, smell, taste, hear, feel.

Write down anything that feels in any way remarkable or noteworthy. This is the kind of detail that, when you review your entries over a series of days, may reveal spiritual movement. It does not have to have cosmic significance. You could write, for example: "The house is so quiet, and I feel so comfortable wrapped in my prayer shawl."

This is as good a place as any to point out that you are not writing for anyone but yourself. As someone trained in correct writing, it took me a while to get over the idea that my spelling, punctuation, and grammar had to be perfect. That kind of concern has its place, but not in journal-writing. Make up words. Use your own personal shorthand or abbreviations that no one else would understand. Reference memories without explaining them. Your journal is for your eyes only.

Having done your physical inventory, acknowledge what your mind is doing. Many of us enter prayer time already thinking about what we are going to do when our prayers are done. Or there may be an issue that has been occupying our thinking. Again, it is helpful to acknowledge that whatever is currently on your mind is part of your life today, but you only need note this in your journal if it feels significant.

From attending to mental activity, we now turn to the heart of the matter. If your physical and mental inventories didn't generate anything you care to write about, here is where you want to begin writing. What is on your heart today? We use the expression, "My heart went out..." To what or whom has your heart gone out in the last day? About what or whom have you been praying? Most of us will pray for people in crisis, but we also typically pray for our loved ones even when, by the grace of God, they are happy and healthy. If this is the case, hold these people in your heart and feel your love extending out to them.

Now, remember Jesus asking the blind man, "What do you want me to do for you?" (Mark 10:51). Imagine Jesus asking you personally, referencing everything upon which you have reflected and written today, "What do you want me to do for you?" Think carefully about this and write your response in your journal. It is better to address Jesus directly here, as if you were talking to him, rather than writing something like "If Jesus asked me what I wanted, this is what I would tell him."

Then, sit in silence for a few moments and listen for Jesus' reply. Bear in mind that Jesus does not always speak in words, and that his answer may only reveal itself over an extended period, possibly days after you have articulated your prayer. But if you do perceive an immediate answer to your prayer, that's certainly worth recording!

PART I
PRELUDE

WEEK 1

YOUR DAILY PRAYER TIME

SWEET HOUR OF PRAYER

William Walford (1772-1850)

Sweet hour of prayer, sweet hour of prayer,

That calls me from a world of care,

And bids me at my Father's throne

Make all my wants and wishes known.

In seasons of distress and grief

My soul has often found relief.

And oft escaped the tempter's snare

By thy return, sweet hour of prayer.

Sweet hour of prayer, sweet hour of prayer,

Thy wings shall my petition bear

To Him whose truth and faithfulness

Engage the waiting soul to bless;

And since He bids me seek His face,

Believe His word and trust His grace,

I'll cast on Him my ev'ry care,

And wait for thee, sweet hour of prayer.

Lift Every Voice and Sing II: An African American Hymnal (New York: Church Publishing, 1993), 178.

The exercises this week will acquaint you (or reacquaint you) with forms of prayer that support the exercises in the coming chapters. Each exercise this week asks you to focus a different form of prayer. As the exercises unfold for you in the coming weeks, you will probably use a combination of these forms to make up your daily prayer time.

DISPOSITION TO PRAYER

For most of us, transitioning from any kind of activity into prayer requires some intentionality. Your mind and spirit will pick up cues from your physical situation. If you consciously arrange your body in a prayerful attitude, it will become more natural to pray with your mind and spirit as well. Pay attention to your physical space. As far as possible, seek a quiet place. Ask the people you live with not to interrupt you for an hour or so.

Surround yourself with things that inspire you to prayerfulness. If possible, dedicate a part of your living quarters as your prayer space. You might use a small table or shelf as a home altar and put on it objects that are holy to you. A cross, icons, candles, and incense are obvious choices, but you may also place anything that makes you feel closer to God. A friend of mine has a habit of placing on her home altar articles she finds on her daily walks: a wildflower, a snakeskin, or a deer's antler.

You may want a prayer rug or kneeler, but a cushion or a plain chair is fine too. Try not to use the same chair you use for work, however. Keep your Bible and this book within reach.

Pay attention to your physical posture. Your position should be comfortable enough for you to maintain it for 20 minutes or so, but not so comfortable that you fall asleep. Many people find this involves a straight back with feet flat on the floor.

Many people enjoy playing music to prepare for prayer. Begin with a rote prayer if you like, like the Our Father or the Serenity Prayer. Do what feels right for you. Feel God's welcome.

PRAYER EXERCISES

As you begin each day's exercise, in this chapter and all that follow:

- Dispose yourself for prayer as described above.

- Breathe deeply, at least one cleansing breath.

- Pray for the grace of the week.

- Read through the entire day's prompt before beginning the first step.

This week, the *grace* is:

Joy and peace in the discipline of daily prayer.

DAY 1: JOURNALING WITH THE NINETEENTH ANNOTATION

If you did the journaling exercise at the end of the preceding chapter, you will be acquainted with one general method of journaling. Today we apply that method to the specific format of the Nineteenth Annotation as presented in this book. This exercise is especially geared to people who have not journaled before, or who have had trouble journaling.

The first thing, as in the exercise at the end of the introduction, is to get something down so that you are not staring at that most intimidating of spectacles, a blank page. In your journal, after writing the date and day of the week, write down "Part 1, Week 1: Your Daily Prayer Time, Day 1." (Obviously, the title and the number of the chapter will change every week, and the day will change every day.)

For most of his meditations, Ignatius asks the exercitant to consider the "place" and the "grace." For me, it is most helpful to begin with the grace. So below your Bible reference, copy out the grace suggested for that day. For this week, of course, you would write: "Grace: joy and peace in the discipline of daily prayer."

Most of your daily exercises begin with a Bible reference. Today we use Habakkuk 2:1-3. Note the citation in your journal and then read the passage.

This passage is short, so you can, if you like, copy the entire reference into your journal. But a few words are sufficient if they call the passage to mind when you go back and reread your entry. In this case, you might just enter, "Write the vision."

Now, imagine the "place." In some of your Bible passages, the "place" is a physical location, like a street in Jerusalem. In others, the "place" is more abstract. If that is the case, you will have to rely on your emotional imagination rather than your sensory imagination. What feelings arise when you think about the thematic context of your passage?

In the case of Habakkuk 2:1-3, you might imagine the prophet standing at his "watchpost" waiting for God to speak. What are his feelings? Anticipation? Hope? Dread? Can you identify with Habakkuk in any of these emotions?

Hear God's response to Habakkuk: "write the vision." Imagine these words directed at yourself. If God asked you to "write the vision," what would you write? Write this in your journal. If it is just, "I don't know what to say. Please, God, tell me what you want me to say," you will understand something of what a prophet apparently experiences.

Write about anything you have perceived or learned. How does this day's exercise fit into your life right now? Could it be an answer to whatever you have asked of Jesus?

If this exercise has been helpful, in the coming weeks, use the same basic formula in journaling: Begin with the data (date, week, day, etc.) and then the grace of the week and your scripture reference. You will find these headings helpful when you review your journal, as you will be called to do at the end of each week. If after recording your headings, you write honestly about anything at all that is on your mind or heart, you are fine.

DAY 2: CENTERING PRAYER

Many people think of prayer as talking to God. Prayers of praise, intercession, supplication, confession, and thanksgiving typically fall into this category. In centering prayer, by contrast, the emphasis is on *listening* to God, experiencing God's presence within oneself through the cultivation of interior silence. Practitioners of centering prayer will often set a timer for 20 minutes in which to remain silent, still, and open. As thoughts enter the mind, as they inevitably will, they are gently set aside. Many people find the use of a "sacred word" helpful. This is a word or short phrase used to restore interior quietness when your mind wanders. Some portion of the time set aside for the daily exercises is often profitably spent in centering prayer.[8]

Today's scripture reference is Psalm 46:10a.

To begin today's exercise:

- Dispose yourself for prayer as described above.
- Breathe deeply, at least one cleansing breath.
- Pray for the grace of the week.
- Read through the entire day's prompt before beginning the first step.
- Set a timer (the one on your phone or watch is ideal). If you have never practiced centering prayer before, start with five minutes, and see if you can lengthen

---

[8] For more on centering prayer see Cynthia Bourgeault, *Centering Prayer and Inner Awakening* (Cambridge: Cowley, 2004) and almost anything by Thomas Keating.

your prayer time by a minute each week until you can sit quietly for 20 minutes.

- Repeat to yourself Psalm 46:10a: "Be still and know that I am God!" If you prefer, use Merrill's version of this half-verse: "Be still and know that I am Love."[9] Say the first part, "Be still and know" while breathing in and the second part, "that I am God!" on the exhale. Listen to the silence and become aware of God's nearness. When your mind wanders, repeat your verse.

Do not self-evaluate and worry about doing it wrong. Any time spent with God is exactly right. One wise teacher told me to be grateful for those irresistible little ideas that capture your mind because each one is an opportunity to return your attention to God.

DAY 3: LECTIO DIVINA

Lectio Divina, Latin for "sacred reading," is an ancient way of reading the Bible devotionally. The fancy name belies a simple process of reading a Bible passage three times: first for surface meaning, then for what it evokes for you personally, and then to consider how God may be calling you. Finally, you offer your reflections to God in prayer. Since Bible readings accompany most exercises in the weeks that follow, this is a useful practice to master.

Today as an example, we will use Mark 1:16-20.

- Dispose yourself for prayer as described above.
- Breathe deeply, at least one cleansing breath.
- Pray for the grace of the week.

---

[9] Merrill, *Psalms for Praying*, 88.

- Read through the entire day's prompt before beginning the first step.

- First read the passage for meaning. If you like, read it aloud. What is this passage about? On a basic level, Mark 1:16-20 is a story about Jesus calling his first disciples.

- Read the passage again slowly. Which words or phrases arrest your attention? These could be words you stumble over or words that attract you. Copy the words down in your journal. How do these words affect you? Are they comforting or challenging? Why do you think they are resonating with you today? Is there something in your current situation or your past that relates? In the case of this passage, you might reflect on what Jesus' call has felt like in your own life.

- Reread the passage one last time. What does God have to say to you personally today through this passage?

- Respond to God in prayer and/or in your journal.

DAY 4: IMAGINATIVE PRAYER

Imaginative prayer, a prominent feature of Ignatian spirituality, is especially effective with the parts of the Bible that tell stories, like the shepherds keeping watch in their fields by night, the wedding feast at Cana, or Jesus' Passion in Jerusalem. Read the story carefully, then reimagine the scene as if personally present. Take the role of any participant: one of the disciples, a person asking for healing, or even Jesus himself. Or be a nameless bystander or a "fly on the wall," simply observing the action. As you imagine the action unfolding, pay particular attention to your emotional or spiritual state. Do not be at all concerned with what you "should" be feeling. Record your imagined experience honestly in your journal. Over time, reviewing your journal entries will give you an idea of how you are moving spiritually.

For today, let's try imaginative prayer with John 5:2-9.

• Dispose yourself for prayer as described above.

• Breathe deeply, at least one cleansing breath.

• Pray for the grace of the week.

• Read through the entire day's prompt before beginning the first step.

• Read the passage slowly and imagine the place. In this case, there is a physical place to imagine. You are there, in Jerusalem, at the Sheep Gate. Are there sheep there? Is it hot or cool? Sunny or overcast? Are you walking, standing, or sitting? On what kind of surface? What do the porticoes and pool look like? What do the beggars look like, smell like?

• From here on, you have a choice as to the role you are to play. It may be easiest to begin by pretending to be a bystander, but the exercise is often profitably repeated in the roles of people mentioned or implied in the story: the beggar with whom Jesus speaks, or one of the other beggars, or a disciple, or Jesus himself (no, it's not sacrilegious to do this!)

• Use your five senses. What do you see, hear, smell, taste and feel? Hear the conversation. Note the expressions on faces. Especially note how you feel as an observer or participant. Let the action unfold as described in the passage. Something may happen in your imagination that is not described in the Bible story. That is fine. Simply take note of this if it happens.

- Do not hurry through this, but when the time seems right to you, gently remove yourself from first-century Jerusalem and return to your current situation. What sticks in your mind? What might it mean about you? What might God be trying to tell you through your imagined experience? These are all good things to record in your journal. Offer your reflections to God in prayer.

DAY 5: THE EXAMEN

The examen was briefly described in the introduction. Today's exercise will be an opportunity for you to practice the examen during your daily prayer time.

- Dispose yourself for prayer as described above.
- Breathe deeply, at least one cleansing breath.
- Pray for the grace of the week.
- Read through the entire day's prompt before beginning the first step.
- To begin, consider first God's great love for you but also consider what you are bringing to God. Pay particular attention to the gifts God has given you:

your unique constellation of interests, aptitudes, talents. Consider that God loves what makes you you.

• Place yourself in the context of God's love by imagining you are greeting a beloved relative or friend, especially after an absence. What is the first thing you do? You embrace, possibly kiss, smile, and gaze at each other. Experience the intense feelings of such an encounter. See if you can translate that joy into the idea of God welcoming you into prayer. God loves to meet people in prayer.

> It is okay to imagine God with the face of your beloved (remembering that your beloved is not God, of course!). Appearing with the face of the beloved is something God does all the time.

• From here, thanksgiving is a natural segue. Your host says, "Thank you so much for coming!" and you reply, "Thanks so much for having me!" Here you are talking to God, so thank God for whatever else comes to mind: your gifts, your family and your health, the sunshine (or the rain), security, your vocation.

• Now ask God to bless you with the ability to be honest with yourself and with God. Try to look at yourself without self-delusion or ego.

• Review the last day. You can do this hour by hour, if that helps, or you can allow the strongest memories of the last day to emerge, paying special attention to sensory impressions and feelings. When were you happiest, freest, most at home with yourself, closest to God? When were you most anxious, annoyed, out-of-sorts, furthest from God? Recall what led up to these experiences. What part did your own attitudes or actions play, if any?

- Were there any instances of your thinking or behaving in a way that is inconsistent with being God's beloved child? If so, now is the time to name them. Do not self-flagellate or wallow in a vague sense of not being "good enough." Try to name the specific commandment or teaching from which you have strayed. Honestly recognize any genuine fault and renew your commitment to follow in God's ways. Be assured that God forgives repented wrongdoing. Rest in that forgiveness.

- The whole point of the examen is renewal. If you have identified something for which you asked forgiveness, now ask for the grace to respond differently next time similar circumstances present. It is helpful if you have identified a fault to ask for the corresponding grace. For example, if you caught yourself being impatient, ask for patience.

- Rest in God. Listen.

- Before you end your examen, thank God for your prayer, and consciously receive benediction.

- If desired, journal your experience.

A caution: Unfortunately, for many people, the examen can simply become a daily confession, often of the same sins, day after day after day. This can block the flow of renewal. To avoid this pitfall, never neglect the prelude, situating yourself in God's love. Everything in the spiritual life begins and ends in the love of God.

DAY 6: THE EXAMEN

Reading:

> *You can relax now*
>
> *C'mon and open your eyes*
>
> *Breathe deeply now*
>
> *I am with you*
>
> *Oh my sweet, sweet child*
>
> *Who do you think you are?*
>
> *You are the child of God*
>
> *And that will never change.*
>
> *You had a dream, you misunderstood*
>
> *You thought we were separate*
>
> *But now you hear my voice and*
>
> *You can relax now*
>
> *C'mon and open your eyes*
>
> *Breathe deeply now*
>
> *I am with you*
>
> *You are the love of my life*
>
> *You are my one creation*

You are eternity

And that will never change.[10]

Susan McCullen's poem, which has been set to music by Shaina Noll, evokes the essence of the examen. In the spirit of this gentle lyric, repeat yesterday's examen exercise during your daily prayer time today.

Beginning next week, set aside some time to do your examen independently of your daily prayer at a time that is mostly likely to become habitual for you. Continue to use this song or any other poetry that helps you with your daily examen.

DAY 7: REPETITION

Ignatius calls for a periodic review of recent exercises, which he calls "repetition." This is an opportunity to discern movement that might not be apparent from day to day. Without repetition, we may be unaware in the daily distractions of life of how God is working in us. When we recognize how active God has been in our growth, we are energized to continue the journey.

This is one reason I have put so much emphasis on journaling. If we keep a record of where we have been, we can more clearly see God's movement within us. We become more aware of God's myriad gifts. Trends become apparent, so we have a clearer idea of where God may be leading. With the perspective of time, we can better see what is important and what is distracting.

Review your experience over the last week. Reread your journal and highlight what has been most important, enlightening, disturbing, moving. Is there something that has stayed with you? Something in the chapter

---

[10] "You Can Relax Now." Words by Susan McCullen, susanmccullen.com. Used by permission. For a lovely musical rendition, search "Shaina Noll You Can Relax Now" on YouTube.com.

heading, the grace, or one of the scripture lessons? Was there something toward which you felt resistance? Have you noticed patterns in your behavior and prayer when you do your examen? What do these perceptions tell you about yourself? What do they reveal about God? Pay particular attention to your state of mind and heart. When were you joyful? Confident? Anxious? Sorrowful? When did you feel closest to or farthest from God?

How does any of this relate to your life right now: your family, your job, your actions and attitudes? Can you recall any "real-life" experiences in the past week that relate to the exercises? What might God be communicating to you?

Do not expect the earth to shake every week. God's work within us is sometimes subtle. Remember that the Nineteenth Annotation takes time. Daily and even weekly changes may be difficult to notice. But do not doubt that God is at work within you. God is generous. You are loved and gifted.

WEEK 2

FIRST PRINCIPLES

THE CREATION

James Weldon Johnson (1871-1938)

And God stepped out on space,
And he looked around and said:
I'm lonely—
I'll make me a world.

And far as the eye of God could see
Darkness covered everything,
Blacker than a hundred midnights
Down in a cypress swamp.

Then God smiled,
And the light broke,
And the darkness rolled up on one side,
And the light stood shining on the other,
And God said: That's good!

Then God reached out and took the light in his hands,
And God rolled the light around in his hands
Until he made the sun;
And he set that sun a-blazing in the heavens.
And the light that was left from making the sun
God gathered it up in a shining ball

And flung it against the darkness,

Spangling the night with the moon and stars.

Then down between

The darkness and the light

He hurled the world;

And God said: That's good!

Then God himself stepped down—

And the sun was on his right hand,

And the moon was on his left;

The stars were clustered about his head,

And the earth was under his feet.

And God walked, and where he trod

His footsteps hollowed the valleys out

And bulged the mountains up.

Then he stopped and looked and saw

That the earth was hot and barren.

So God stepped over to the edge of the world

And he spat out the seven seas—

He batted his eyes, and the lightnings flashed—

He clapped his hands, and the thunders rolled—

And the waters above the earth came down,

The cooling waters came down.

Then the green grass sprouted,

And the little red flowers blossomed,

The pine tree pointed his finger to the sky,

And the oak spread out his arms,

The lakes cuddled down in the hollows of the ground,

And the rivers ran down to the sea;

And God smiled again,

And the rainbow appeared,

And curled itself around his shoulder.

Then God raised his arm and he waved his hand

Over the sea and over the land,

And he said: Bring forth! Bring forth!

And quicker than God could drop his hand,

Fishes and fowls

And beasts and birds

Swam the rivers and the seas,

Roamed the forests and the woods,

And split the air with their wings.

And God said: That's good!

Then God walked around,

And God looked around

On all that he had made.

He looked at his sun,

And he looked at his moon,

And he looked at his little stars;

He looked on his world

With all its living things,

And God said: I'm lonely still.

Then God sat down—

On the side of a hill where he could think;

By a deep, wide river he sat down;

With his head in his hands,

God thought and thought,

Till he thought: I'll make me a man!

Up from the bed of the river

God scooped the clay;

And by the bank of the river

He kneeled him down;

And there the great God Almighty

Who lit the sun and fixed it in the sky,

Who flung the stars to the most far corner of the night,

Who rounded the earth in the middle of his hand;

This great God,

Like a mammy bending over her baby,

Kneeled down in the dust

Toiling over a lump of clay

Till he shaped it in is his own image;

Then into it he blew the breath of life,

And man became a living soul.

Amen.   Amen.

James Weldon Johnson, God's Trombones: Seven Negro Sermons in Verse (Penguin Classics, 2008), 15-17.

"I believe in One God..."

So begins the Apostles' Creed. These words are spoken by a person being baptized, or by parents, godparents, and sponsors on the baptismal candidate's behalf. So begins one's life as a Christian.

These are words with consequences. Sooner or later, if we are to not only identify as Christians but live as Christians, we must make decisions that reflect that identity. "What sort of persons ought you to be in leading lives of holiness and godliness?" asks the author of 2 Peter.

Ignatius finds the answers to questions like this in basic theology. God made the world. God made human beings and called them to participate in the world's ongoing creation and re-creation. God made all kinds of beautiful and helpful things to support that calling. How then shall we live? We try to live in a way to model these beliefs.

This is what Ignatius says:

God freely created us so that we might know, love, and serve him in this life and be happy with him forever. God's purpose in creating us is to draw forth from us a response of love and service here on earth, so we may attain our goal of everlasting happiness with him in heaven.

All the things in this world are gifts of God, created for us, to be the means by which we can come to know him better, love him more surely, and serve him more faithfully.

As a result, we ought to appreciate and use these gifts of God insofar as they help us toward our goal of loving service and union with God. But insofar as any created things hinder our progress toward our goal, we ought to let them go.

In everyday life, then, we should keep ourselves indifferent or undecided in the face of all created gifts when we have an option and we do not have the clarity of what would be a better choice. We ought not to be led on by our natural likes and dislikes even in matters such as health or sickness, wealth, or poverty...

Rather, our only desire and our one choice should be that option which better leads us to the goal for which God created us.[11]

Ignatius calls this his "First Principle and Foundation" and builds all his Exercises upon it. This basic premise must be understood for the exercises that follow to make sense.

At the same time, the First Principle may be challenging. As a spiritual director, I particularly encounter resistance around Ignatius' concept of indifference. Many people react negatively to this word, perhaps only because the word itself is a negative. Freedom, on the other hand, is a positive concept, and at this point in your exercises, I invite your reflection on it as an alternative.

God created human beings to be free. God wants creation to be free. God wants us to be free of all attachments that limit our ability to love God and love others.

---

[11] David L. Fleming, *The Spiritual Exercises of Saint Ignatius: A Literal Translation & A Contemporary Reading* (St. Louis: Institute of Jesuit Sources, 1991), 23.

Attachments come in various forms. The classic human attachments are money and material goods, approval and fame, power. Food, drugs, and unhealthy relationships are other examples. What they have in common is that they lack the ability to ultimately satisfy. At best, eventually they disappoint or become boring. At worst, they destroy.

Ironically, all attachments grow out of a desire for goodness. Even addictive drugs initially make a person feel good.

But human beings are like gasoline engines. Gasoline engines are made to run on a particular fuel. Put something else in their tanks, like kerosene or diesel, and they don't work. They may even explode.

PRAYER EXERCISES

- Dispose yourself for prayer.

- Breathe deeply, at least one cleansing breath.

- Pray for the grace of the week.

- Read through the entire day's prompt before beginning the first step.

- Practice *lectio divina* with the scripture passages.

- Journal your answers to each day's prayer prompts, or otherwise as moved.

- Offer your reflections to God in prayer.

- Remember to do your examen some time before bed

This week, the *grace* is:

To know myself as beloved of God.

DAY 1: GOD CREATED THE COSMOS FROM LOVE

And God stepped out on space,

And he looked around and said:

I'm lonely—

I'll make me a world.

~Excerpt from The Creation by James Weldon Johnson (1871-1938)[13]

Scripture: John 1:1-5; Psalm 148

Love is by nature creative. Wherever there is love, something is born, lives and grows. What we call creation is itself born from the love of God, which is so great it had to overflow into the material world. We are all familiar with the phrase, "God so loved the world…," but what if we thought of God's love being the foundation of the entire universe? How does this concept compare with your own worldview? As you go through your day, try to recall that God's love underpins everything you see.

DAY 2: GOD CREATED HUMANKIND FROM LOVE

This great God,

Like a mammy bending over her baby,

Kneeled down in the dust

Toiling over a lump of clay

Till he shaped it in is his own image;

Then into it he blew the breath of life,

---

[13] James Weldon Johnson, "The Creation," *God's Trombones: Seven Negro Sermons in Verse* (New York: Penguin Classics, 2008), 15.

And man became a living soul.

Amen.   Amen.

~Excerpt from The Creation by James Weldon Johnson (1871-1938)[14]

Scripture: Genesis 1:26-31; Genesis 2:4-7, 21-23

What does it mean to be created in God's image? What does it mean to know you have God's very breath in your lungs? See if you can express that to God. As you become aware of your breathing throughout the course of your day, be conscious that God is breathing through you.

DAY 3: GOD CREATED HUMANS FOR LOVE

There is no remedy for love but to love more.

~Henry David Thoreau

Scripture: John 15:12-13; 1 John 4:7-12

Take a moment to bring to mind, one by one, the people who have loved you and the people you love. You may want to list them in your journal. Picture these people, remember how each one of them says/said your name. Take note of how you feel as you think of each one. How is God present in in the loves of your life? Offer that love to God.

---

[14] Johnson, "Creation," 17.

DAY 4: GOD CREATED ME

Scripture: Psalm 139:1-18; Isaiah 43:1, 3

Consider the wonder of being God's creation. Pray to see yourself as God sees you. What happens when you look at someone you love deeply? Can you imagine God looking at you that way? How would your self-image change if you were to look at God looking at you? Would your image of God change?

DAY 5: GOD CREATED ME FOR LOVE

Scripture: 1 Corinthians 12: 4-11

God created you to love in two senses. The first is that God created you that God might have you to love, the same way loving human parents create a baby so that they might love it. The second is that God created you to be a loving person that you might love, and to use your gifts in the service of love. As you read 1 Corinthians 12, consider what gifts God has given you. You might have some of the gifts St. Paul mentions, and you might have some gifts he does not. Record your gifts and potential gifts in your journal. Rejoice in being a gifted person. Say a prayer offering your gifts to God's service.

DAY 6: GOD CREATED ME FOR FREEDOM

Scripture: Genesis 1:28-30; 1 Corinthians 6:12

When in your life have you felt most free? Call to mind these experiences and try to feel the freedom anew. What do these experiences have in common? Now try to think of times when you have felt less freedom. What were they like? Finally, do a careful self-examination of your life now. In what ways are you not completely free? What impedes your freedom? Are there adjustments to your actions or attitudes that might result in greater freedom? Offer these reflections to God with a prayer for the full freedom God intends for you.

Conclude by imagining God's great love enveloping you. You may wish to wrap yourself in a blanket or shawl to bring the idea home.

DAY 7: REPETITION

Review the last week, rereading your journal entries. Then, drawing upon what you now feel to be true about the world, God, and yourself, write your own "First Principle and Foundation."

A PRAYER HABIT

You are called into a relationship with God that underpins and enlightens every aspect of your life. In addition to the time you consciously dedicate to prayer, there are habits you can cultivate that enforce a life of prayer, that you may, more and more, "pray without ceasing" (1 Thessalonians 5:17). Here is one:

Set your day on a righteous course before you even get out of bed in the morning. Imagine the day ahead, ask God's blessing on your plans, and pray that all you do and say this day may reflect God's love and glory. Pray that the grace of the week may be manifest to you.

PART II

POWERLESSNESS AND RESPONSIBILITY

PSALM 56

Nan C. Merrill

Be gracious to me, O Merciful Love,

for I dread the power of others;

all day long my fears consume me;

I am like a door mat that people step upon;

to oppose another's will seems too much for me.

Now, when I am afraid, I put my trust in You.

In You, O Guide and Comforter, I find the strength to act.

What can others do to me?

Too often I succumb to invitations not in my best interest;

I do that which I know can only lead to harm.

Others know of my weakness; they watch my downfall.

Only with You by my side, O Rock,

will I find courage to choose new life.

In your saving grace, answer my prayer, O Beloved!

If You had kept count of my transgressions,

Your tears could fill a lake!

Are they not in your book?

Now my fears will be turned back,

in the day when I call.

This I know, that the Beloved dwells within.

in the Holy One, whose Light I praise,

In You shall I trust without fear.

What can others do to me?

My vows to You I must uphold, O Beloved;

I give You thanks; my heart overflows with gratitude.

For You deliver me from the depths of despair.

Yes, my fears You help me to face;

they are put to rest,

That I may walk with You, O Beloved,

into the light of a new dawn.

"In the beginning, God created the heavens and the earth…"

So begins the Holy Bible, Genesis Chapter 1, verse 1. The refrain after each stage of creation is some variation on "it was good." In the Judeo-Christian world, the premise that God created the world and human beings to be good is absolutely foundational. How then can it be, as anyone with eyes can see, that many things are very bad?

The Bible explains this problem by describing how sin entered the world almost immediately after Creation was completed. By Chapter 3 of Genesis, we are reading about the first man and first woman disobeying God to eat fruit from the one tree God has forbidden to them. Whether or not you believe that these events materially happened just as described in Genesis, there is truth here: Sin has been with humankind from the beginning.

In the last chapter, we explored the good and beautiful origins of the world, of human beings, and of ourselves. Before we go on, if our beliefs are to have relevance in the real world, we need to steer into the reality of sin.

Ignatius, in his wisdom, realized this, and placed the consideration of sin in "Week 1" of his Exercises. His purpose is not that we should wallow in guilt but that we recognize two things: our responsibility for our own actions, and our utter dependence on God.

These two things are not, as may appear at first blush, mutually exclusive. Human beings are creative agents, not automatons or slaves. Christianity teaches that we assume responsibility for our own actions and accept the consequences. At the same time, we are finite, mortal, and fallible. The ability to choose and accomplish always the right thing lies beyond our abilities. We are susceptible through our appetites, imaginations, and egos to temptation. We are prone to substitute incomplete or temporary goods for the greater goods that God prepares for us. Ultimately the desire to be good by our own efforts fails. We are completely dependent on God.

One person who recognized this truth centuries after Ignatius was Bill Wilson, founder of Alcoholics Anonymous. The Twelve Steps of Alcoholics Anonymous show the interplay between the recognition of powerlessness and the assumption of responsibility.

THE TWELVE STEPS

1. *We admitted we were powerless over alcohol - that our lives had become unmanageable.*

2. *Came to believe that a Power greater than ourselves could restore us to sanity.*

3. *Made a decision to turn our will and our lives over to the care of God as we understood Him.*

4. *Made a searching and fearless moral inventory of ourselves.*

5. *Admitted to God, to ourselves and to another human being the exact nature of our wrongs.*

6. *Were entirely ready to have God remove all these defects of character.*

7. *Humbly asked Him to remove our shortcomings.*

8. *Made a list of all persons we had harmed, and became willing to make amends to them all.*

9. *Made direct amends to such people wherever possible, except when to do so would injure them or others.*

10. *Continued to take personal inventory and when we were wrong promptly admitted it.*

11. *Sought through prayer and meditation to improve our conscious contact with God as we understood Him, praying only for knowledge of His will for us and the power to carry that out.*

12. *Having had a spiritual awakening as the result of these steps, we tried to carry this message to alcoholics and to practice these principles in all our affairs.*

Steps 1, 2, 3, 7, and 11 express aspects of the admission of powerlessness. The other steps describe accepting responsibility for the consequences of one's actions: not only past actions while under the influence of alcohol but also on an ongoing basis throughout recovery.

Bill W. realized, as did Ignatius before him, that the combination of admitting powerlessness and accepting responsibility is healing and freeing.

It is in the spirit of healing and freedom that we now consider the effects of sin and evil on the world and on ourselves. For some, this will mean not only the admission of our own sins, but recognition of sin committed against ourselves. Depending on the individual, the latter can be as painful (or more so) than the former. Any unresolved grief, guilt, or shame should be taken up with your spiritual director.

The important thing is to be as honest as you can. Just as in the last chapter, we are trying to see as God sees. Some people, in reviewing their experience with sin, will begin to see that something for which they had always assumed guilt was, in fact, a case of being sinned against. On the other hand, some people who remember being the innocent victim will begin to see their own part in contributing to a dysfunctional and hurtful situation.

Just remember, God is love, and God is in the redemption business. God's capacity for forgiveness is huge. Furthermore, God wastes nothing. Anything about which you are prepared to see greater truth will be used by God to fulfill God's purpose for you. Anything about which you are prepared to see greater truth will, in fact, be used by God to fulfill God's plan of redemption for the world.

PRAYER EXERCISES

- Dispose yourself for prayer.
- Breathe deeply, at least one cleansing breath.
- Pray for the grace of the week.
- Read through the entire day's prompt before beginning the first step.

- Practice *lectio divina* with the scripture passages.

- Journal your answers to each day's prayer prompts, or otherwise as you are moved.

- Offer your reflections to God in prayer.

- Do not forget to do your daily examen sometime before bed.

WEEK 3

SIN IN THE WORLD

This week, the *grace* is:

To acknowledge with sorrow the evil and injustice in God's good world and take comfort in God's mercy.

DAY 1: SIN IS EVERYWHERE

Scripture: Ecclesiastes 1:8-9; Romans 5:12-14

Always remember in our consideration of sin that God created the world out of love to be good, and that darkness, no matter how ubiquitous, cannot overcome God's light.

Have you ever read the news and felt a sense of hopelessness or despair at the evidence of sin in the world? You may wish to note a recent example in your journal.

Consider how recoiling from a perception of evil compares with recoiling from any kind of pain. The sensation of pain is often necessary for us to avoid greater catastrophe. For example, when you touch a hot pan, the sensation of burning causes you to withdraw your hand before it can be more seriously injured. Could your horror at the evidence of sin have any ultimately beneficial effect?

Bring your feelings on this subject into the light of God's presence and ask for grace in dealing with your awareness of sin.

DAY 2: THE INTERCONNECTION OF CREATION

Scripture: Genesis 1:31; Romans 5:18-25

By ascribing the creation of the world to a single hand, the Bible describes the interconnection of all creation. This interconnection is confirmed by modern ecological studies. Damage done in one environment reverberates around the globe. Likewise, human interaction sometimes results in consequences for people not directly involved. What we do affects other people, often in unforeseen and unforeseeable ways.

Sinful acts, just like acts of generosity and grace, can have a ripple effect. Have your acts and attitudes ever had an unintended effect on others? Or have you ever borne the consequences of someone else's actions? When you think about these things, what do your feelings tell you about the interrelatedness of creation?

If we can hurt each other without even meaning to, it can seem as if we are powerless against sin. What difference might it make if we admitted this powerlessness before God?

DAY 3: THE SIN OF THE ANGELS

Scripture: Isaiah 14:12-15

Do you believe in angels? Judeo-Christian scripture and tradition hold that angels are an order of beings higher than humans. What do you think angels are? You don't have to answer that question conclusively to derive some fruit from the story of the angels' rebellion.

What does it mean if even highly placed creatures can fall prey to pride and try to usurp God's authority? What are some ways that people put themselves in God's place? In what ways have you put yourself in God's place? What was the result?

DAY 4: THE SIN OF ADAM AND EVE

Scripture: Genesis 3:1-13, 21

Which was the greater sin? That Adam and Eve disobeyed God, or that they hid from God afterwards, making excuses and blaming each other? How does failure to take responsibility for sin make it worse? Have you ever failed to take responsibility for something done badly? How did that feel? If you are able, admit your responsibility and contemplate a blanket of God's mercy around you. Remember that God provided clothes for Adam and Eve after they sinned.

DAY 5: HELL

Scripture: Matthew 13:41-42; Psalm 22:1-18

Which of these two passages better describe hell for you? Is hell only a place bad people go when they die? What is hell for you?

Have you ever felt cast out of the love of God? How did that feeling come about? If you feel you are in hell now, please speak to your spiritual director. But if you no longer feel that way, what happened to release you?

Read the rest of Psalm 22, verses 19-31. Reflect and journal.

DAY 6: INTRODUCTION TO THE COLLOQUY

The colloquy is made by speaking exactly as one friend speaks to another, ... now asking him for a favor, now [confessing] some misdeed, now making known his affairs to him, and seeking advice in them (SE 54).[15]

---

[15] Ignatius, *Exercises*, 24.

Scripture: Isaiah 1:18; John 15:15

The colloquy is a conversational form of prayer recommended in Ignatius' Spiritual Exercises. In various places, Ignatius encourages such conversations with the Father, with Jesus, and with the Virgin Mary, Mother of Christ. It may be helpful to imagine God the Father, Jesus, Mary, or the Holy Spirit sitting beside you or opposite you. Or you may wish to write your conversation in your journal in the form of a sort of play. Address your companion with your inquiry or concern, and imagine a response. This is a very effective form of prayer for those who tend to put distance between themselves and God.

Today, invite Jesus into conversation and share what is on your mind and heart, asking a favor, sharing some news, confessing a sin, seeking advice, or thanking him for life and for his mercy. Imagine his reply. Close with an *Our Father* and imagine Jesus saying the words with you. After all, he invented them.

DAY 7: REPETITION

Review the last week, rereading your journal entries. What in the prayer prompts or scripture readings stands out for you? What made the deepest impression? What are you feeling at this point about admitting powerlessness? Return to the places of deepest grace that you experienced this week. Are you moved to go deeper? How? Thank God for any graces received this week.

WEEK 4

SIN IN MY LIFE

This week, the *grace* is:

To take responsibility for my own sins and take comfort in God's mercy.

DAY 1: THE TEN COMMANDMENTS

Scripture: Exodus 20:1-17

When all else fails, follow the directions. Here we go back to the Ten Commandments, given by God to Moses as a sign of how the people of Israel were to keep covenant with their God.

Review the commandments before entering into prayer. Ask God for a better understanding of the commandments and how they relate to your life with God. Ask also for a spirit of freedom and personal honesty.

As you read each commandment, stop and reflect on how you have been faithful or unfaithful to it. If faithful, move on to the next commandment. If unfaithful, ask and receive forgiveness. You do not have to relive every transgression if previously you have asked and received forgiveness for it. If you have received forgiveness for something, express thanks.

Are there some transgressions you tend to repeat? Ask for amendment of life as well as forgiveness.

DAY 2: THE HUMAN CONDITION

Scripture: Psalm 14:2-4; Romans 7:15-25

Yesterday we considered sin as a violation of a commandment or teaching. Today let us consider "sin" as a condition of human life. No matter how hard we try, we can't seem to be good all the time. Even when we don't mean to, we inflict pain on one another.

I once almost destroyed a friendship by playfully calling someone a "rogue." To me, it was an innocent enough term. For him, it was an insult. I was mystified about why he'd stopped talking to me until we had an opportunity to clear the air and repair the relationship. I remember the occasion as an example of totally unintentional harm on my part.

Human beings are by definition mortal, finite, and limited in understanding; "only human," in fact. We are prone to egotism and temptation. The person who never makes mistakes is probably totally inert.

Today I invite you to consider whether "sin" is not only an individual transgression but a fact of life as we know it. Do you accept this assessment? Why or why not? Must sin be intentional?

DAY 3: SIN AS ALIENATION

Scripture: 1 John 3:9; Ephesians 4:17-24

Implicitly, the Bible defines sin as alienation from God and from one another. If sin is turning away from God, turning toward God reverses alienation and defeats sin. The author of 1 John says those who no longer sin are "born of God." They have reversed their alienation from God and now live in relationship with God.

How is sin a case of alienation from God? Can you think of examples of alienation from God in your own life? How does living in relationship with God overcome alienation? How can approaching God defeat sin?

DAY 4: READY FOR GOD TO REMOVE SIN

Scripture: John 1:29; James 5:15-16

Most of us know well that it is good to turn our sins and other baggage over to God. Sometimes, though, we hang on to our guilt. Is there any unresolved guilt in your life? Consider the possibility of making a formal confession to a priest if this is the case. Give some thought as to what may be standing in the way of your freedom. God is literally waiting to relieve you of that guilt. Are you ready for God to remove your sin?

A prophetic action is one that expresses the word of God in physical form. When you are ready for God to remove your sin, try a prophetic action of your own. Take a bath or splash your face with water or stand outside with arms outstretched, receiving the warmth of the sun (or the falling rain). Rejoice in the sensation of cleanness and freedom. Journal afterwards about your experience.

DAY 5: MAKING AMENDS

Scripture: Matthew 5:23-24; Luke 19: 8-10

Part of taking responsibility is trying to make good on the wrongs you realize you have committed. Sometimes this is not possible, and sometimes, as the Twelve Steps wisely recognize, to try to make amends may do more harm than good. This lack of closure can be hard to deal with. Often a discreet priest or understanding friend can help you understand that God still forgives you even if people do not. It may be helpful to practice another prophetic action to literally *understand* God's forgiveness. Go outside and *stand under* something, like a tree or an umbrella or canopy. Look up and think of God's forgiveness stretching over you in the same way. Journal about your feelings.

If you have identified something for which it is possible to make amends, resolve to do it. Sometimes this is as simple as a phone call or a written note or an anonymous donation on the internet.

DAY 6: PERSONAL INVENTORY

Scripture: James 1:22-25; 2 Corinthians 13:5

Awareness of our own sin is not a "one and done" thing. Few of us are able to confess a transgression, receive forgiveness, and "sin no more." This is why we examine our consciences every day, as thoroughly and fearlessly as we can, and name our sins to God. Fortunately, God's forgiving grace is abundant.

When you look in the mirror, what do you see? In your journal, write a searching description of yourself. Start at the top with your name and "Beloved child of God." List both gifts and weaknesses. Next week, plan to go back and reread what you have written.

Think of your description when you leave the "mirror" and go about your day. Are you able to "remember what you look like"? Under what circumstances is it hardest to remember your true self as a child of God?

DAY 7: REPETITION

Review the last week, rereading your journal entries. What in the prayer prompts or scripture readings stands out for you? What made the deepest impression? What are you feeling at this point about admitting responsibility for your actions?

Did you decide to make amends for anything? How are you doing with that? What are you feeling about that?

Return to the places of deepest grace that you experience this week. Are you moved to go deeper? How? Thank God for any graces received this week.

WEEK 5

MYSELF BEFORE GOD

This week, the *grace* is:

To acknowledge my utter dependance on God.

DAY 1: ANIMA CHRISTI

Ignatius begins his exercises with a prayer called the *Anima Christi*, which is Latin for "Soul of Christ," the opening words. Follows a traditional translation, along with a contemporary rendition by David L. Fleming, S.J. Read them over slowly.

TRADITIONAL

Soul of Christ, sanctify me.

Body of Christ, save me.

Blood of Christ, inebriate me.

Water from the side of Christ, wash me.

Passion of Christ, strengthen me.

O good Jesus, hear me;

Within thy wounds hide me;

Suffer me not to be separated from Thee

From the malignant enemy defend me;

At the hour of my death call me,

And bid me come to thee,

That with thy saints I may praise thee

Forever and ever, Amen.[16]

---

[16] David L. Fleming, *The Spiritual Exercises of St. Ignatius: A Literal Translation & A Contemporary Reading* (St. Louis: Institute of Jesuit Resources, 1980),2.

CONTEMPORARY

Jesus, may all that is you flow into me.

May your body and blood be my food and drink.

May your passion and death be my strength and life.

Jesus, with you by my side enough has been given.

May the shelter I seek be the shadow of your cross.

Let me not run from the love which you offer,

But hold me safe from the forces of evil.

On each of my dyings shed your light and your love.

Keep calling to me until that day comes,

When, with your saints, I may praise you forever. Amen.[17]

Which version do you prefer and why? Which lines attract you, and which lines make you uncomfortable? Why? This is a deeply felt, passionate prayer. Would you be able to pray it with a full heart?

DAY 2: ATTACHMENTS AND FREEDOM

Scripture: Exodus 20:1-6; Matthew 10:37-39

In Week 2, we talked about Ignatius' concept of detachment and how it grows out of a desire to place God first in all things. I offered instead the idea of spiritual freedom. When we feel free is often when we are closest to God and to our true selves.

Still, it is hard to hear Jesus imply that people who love their family members are not worthy to be disciples. It may help to know about a

---

[17] Fleming, *Exercises*, 3.

teaching tool called "rabbinic hyperbole," commonly used by first-century rabbis and with which Jesus was familiar. According to this technique, the teacher grossly exaggerated his point on the theory that even the dullest student would pick up a piece of it. Jesus clearly used this technique on other occasions ("Cut off your hand and throw it away," Matthew 5:30) and is evidently using it here.

The same Jesus who speaks of loving your neighbor as yourself does not turn around and advocate hating our families. In fact, he criticized people who used religious obligations to justify neglecting their parents (Mark 7:11-13). Surely in every truly loving relationship, there is something of God, and God is honored when we honor our relationships.

Fundamentally, this is not a teaching about family relationships anyway. It is a teaching about spiritual freedom. Jesus is concerned that in all things we are always free to love and serve God.

How are you doing with spiritual freedom? Take this opportunity to review once again the areas of your life where you are most free and where you are least free. Are you more or less free than you were three weeks ago when we talked about Ignatius' First Principle? How have your feelings on spiritual freedom evolved?

DAY 3: KENOSIS

Scripture: Philippians 2:5-8; James 4:7

The Godhead emptied itself as a gift to humanity in the form of Jesus Christ. Jesus Christ emptied himself to experience and sanctify the very worst of human suffering and death. Ignatius and many other saints teach self-emptying in the service of God and in imitation of Christ. The theological word for this is *kenosis*, and it figures prominently in Christian spirituality.

Self-emptying is hard enough for a person with a healthy sense of self, but it is problematic for those whose sense of self has been compromised by neglect, violence, or other dehumanizing influences. How is your sense of self? How open are you at this point to the idea of self-emptying to God? Answer as honestly as you can, and don't be concerned if the answer is, "Not much right now." You may have good reasons for your answer. Consider what those reasons might be. Offer them to God in prayer.

We will revisit the idea of self-emptying in solidarity with Christ when we consider his Passion several weeks from now. For the time being, know that God meets you where you are.

DAY 4: SACRIFICE

Scripture: John 15:12-13; Romans 5:6-8

Take a moment to call to mind instances of which you are aware when someone performed a sacrificial act. You might remember Fr. Mychal Judge, who hurried to the World Trade Center on September 11 upon hearing of the attacks and died ministering to the wounded and first responders. Or you might remember incidents closer to home, like a person who gives up a promising career to care for a disabled child or parent, or the health care professionals who care for COVID victims at heightened personal risk. What can prompt such selfless action?

Now think of Christ on the cross. What does that image have in common with the instances of which you have been thinking? What can account for Jesus' willingness to suffer this way? Imagine a colloquy with Jesus in which you ask him this question. What does he say? What is your response?

DAY 5: LIVING TO GOD

Scripture: Romans 12:1-2; Romans 14:7-9

Not many of us will be called to lay down our lives for others, thank God. But what feelings arise in you when you contemplate those who do? Think specifically of Jesus' willingness to suffer, which he offered not so that you would never suffer, but so that you might never be alone in your suffering. How do you respond? We will probably not have to die for Christ, but can we live for Christ? What does living for Christ look like for you?

DAY 6: COLLOQUY OF THANKS

Scripture: Hebrews 13:15-16; Colossians 3:14-17

We have been considering the ubiquity of sin in the world and the presence of sin in ourselves. God's love abides and abounds. "While we were yet sinners," Jesus gave himself for us and continues to give himself, day after day, in himself and in the sacrifices of our fellow humans. If the contemplation of these things has evoked any gratitude in you, express it now. St. Paul encourages the expression of gratitude in music. Is there a song that comes to mind as you think in gratitude of all that God has done for you? Play or sing it now or copy it into your journal as your offering of thanks.

DAY 7: REPETITION

Review the last week, rereading your journal entries and reviewing the prayer prompts and Scripture lessons. Then, drawing upon what you now feel to be true about the world, God, and yourself. write your own version of the *Anima Christe*.

WEEK 6

DISCERNMENT OF GOOD AND EVIL

We've now spent a few weeks acknowledging the effects of sin in the world and on ourselves. We have recognized our responsibility by confession and attempting to make amends, and we have recognized our helplessness and need by turning ourselves over to God's mercy. Now, in order that we may respond to God's invitation to live according to God's ways rather than the ways of sin, we turn to a consideration of recognizing how good and evil forces tend to work in the world and on us. Ignatius made quite a study of this and offers some excellent insights that help when life's choices present themselves.

This week, the *grace* is:

To grow in my ability to discern what is good and what is evil, so that my choices may accord with God's intention and desire for me.

DAY 1: SPIRITS, FORCES, AND THE FALSE SELF.

Sin comes from somewhere. Ignatius speaks of the inner forces that precipitate our thoughts and actions as spirits: the good spirit and the evil spirit. To speak of "spirits" reflects a sixteenth-century cosmology that may seem quaint or archaic to you, but it is a useful shorthand. By observing the effects of sin in the world, we know there are evil forces afoot: racism, aggression, and greed to name a few. These forces, and others like them, work on us internally as well as globally. Often, we are unconscious of them and know them only by their fruits. Ignatius is concerned that we recognize the work of the spirits within us before their prompts translate into sinful thought and action.

As an alternative to referencing "spirits," you may find it helpful to think in terms of the false self and the true self, terminology used by theologians and psychologists alike. For believers, the true self is the image of God placed within human beings from the point of creation. When we are true to ourselves, we conform to God's intent for us and feel content, energized, and at peace with ourselves. When the false self is at work, we feel aggressive, agitated, or hopeless. When an inner voice tells you, "You are worthless; you're not good enough," that is the false self, and you can know this because it contradicts God's word. Alternatively, the false self can say, "You're better than everyone else." You know this is the false self for the same reason.

your truth

Scripture: Ephesians 6:12; Romans 7:15-25   *no regret!*

guilt saves me

In the passage from Romans, Paul describes acting against his own beliefs and later so regretting his actions that he calls himself a wretch. Can you identify? Call a specific instance to mind where you felt similarly. It doesn't have to be something major. Did you eat or drink or play video games or work long hours more than you knew was good for you? Note this in your journal. What were/are your feelings about that? Did you also reach a point where you were convinced you were a bad person? Where are you now with that?

Paul concludes his paragraph by praising Jesus. How did he get there from his previous self-recrimination? What were his intermediate steps? Imagine yourself making a similar transition. How might it affect your feelings about yourself if you were able to move from regret to praise?

DAY 2: STATES OF MIND, BODY, AND SPIRIT

Scripture: Psalm 30:9-10; Luke 6:20-26

These passages describe different mental, spiritual, and physical states. Ignatius, a shrewd observer of human conditions, noted that people react differently to temptation depending on their spiritual state. He observed that the "evil spirit" tempts people who are unconcerned about their sin by offering sensual pleasures and delights to tempt them into further sin, while the "good spirit" appeals to the same people with reason and remorse. Conversely, the evil spirit afflicts people who are aware of their sinfulness with anxiety, sadness, and spiritual disturbance, while the good spirit imparts strength and courage to the same people.

If you have made it this far into the exercises, chances are you are more than sufficiently aware of sin in your life. Has this awareness made you anxious or sad or discouraged you from continuing? What do you make of Ignatius' analysis that this is the evil spirit or the false self? On the other hand, has your awareness of sin made you want to draw closer to God? To what extent are you able at this point to receive strength and accept encouragement to continue? What would the good spirit or your true self be saying to you right now?

DAY 3: CONSOLATION

Reading:

> *I call it consolation when some interior movement in the soul is caused, through which the soul comes to be inflamed with love of its Creator and Lord... I call consolation every increase of hope, faith and charity, and all interior joy which calls and*

attracts to heavenly things and to the salvation of one's soul, quieting it and giving it peace in its Creator and Lord. (SE 316)[18]

In practicing your daily examen, you are already familiar with attending to those experiences in the course of your day when you feel particularly close to God. Along those lines, Ignatius introduces the concept of spiritual consolation as a tool in the discernment of spirits. What resonates with you in the definition of consolation above? When have you known an increase of hope, faith, charity, joy, inner peace, attraction to heavenly things? Describe the experience in your journal.

Be aware that as Ignatius uses the term "consolation," he does not necessarily mean happy times. Even a tragic event can be a consolation if it results in drawing close to God. For example, many persons in recovery from substance abuse look upon "hitting rock bottom" as the beginning of their healing. Have you ever had an unhappy experience in which God drew you close? If so, how does it feel to consider that an experience a consolation?

DAY 4: DESOLATIONS

Reading:

> *I call desolation ... darkness of soul, disturbance in it, movement to things low and earthly, the unquiet of different agitations and temptations, moving to want of confidence, without hope, without love, when one finds oneself all lazy, tepid and sad, and as if separated from his Creator and Lord.* (SE 317)[19]

---

[18] Fleming, *Exercises*, 206.

[19] Fleming, *Exercises*, 206.

When have you experienced spiritual desolation as Ignatius describes it? What helped you recover? Record this in your journal.

Note that just as consolation is not always happy, desolation does not always feel sad, at least at first. Remember from Day 2 of this week that something that appears pleasing or delightful can end up distancing us from God. Have you ever experienced this?

DAY 5: PATTERNS OF SEPARATION

Scripture: Luke 11:24-26; Ephesians 6:13-17

When we recognize the forces that typically separate us from God, we are better able to resist them. Think over the times in your life you have felt most distant from God. What forces were at work? What separates you from God? Where are you most vulnerable? Where are you strongest?

Consider this:

> When one is in desolation, he should be mindful that God has left him to his natural powers to resist the different agitations of the enemy.... He can resist with the help of God, which always remains, though he may not clearly perceive it. For though God has taken from him the abundance of fervor and overflowing love and the intensity of His favors, he has sufficient grace for salvation. (SE 320)[20]

---

[20] Ignatius, *Exercises*, 116.

DAY 6: BEST PRACTICES

Scripture: Psalm 77:11-12; James 5:13-16

Consolation and desolation are natural occurrences in the spiritual life. We do not take credit for the consolations but give glory to God. We do not blame ourselves for desolations but make confession, if necessary, and remain faithful in prayer. Ignatius warns against making changes and new resolutions while in a state of desolation, because in this state, we are more vulnerable to the "evil spirit." Consolation, on the other hand, is an opportunity to store up strength to call upon against future privation.

Reflect on a time of consolation and describe it in detail in your journal. Resolve to return to it when you find yourself in desolation.

DAY 7: REPETITION

One of the reasons journaling is so useful is that, in periodically reviewing our writing, we can recognize patterns in our experience and behavior. By recording our consolations and desolations we learn what brings us closer to God and what distances us. With this knowledge we can, with God's help, modify our behavior in order to remain close to God and avoid the forces that tend to distance us.

Reviewing your journal entries for this period, are there any changes that suggest themselves? If so, pray about them, asking God to confirm them if they accord with God's will. Discuss them with your director. Remember not to make changes when in a state of desolation. If no changes suggest themselves, remain faithful in prayer, and take comfort as always in God's abiding love.

PART III

SEEING, KNOWING, FOLLOWING

NOT POSSIBLE

Cynthia Byers Walter (2014)

The midwife smiled: a perfect child, the bleeding stopped.

Oh, she was right: my perfect brightstar little one—

the seizures can't undo her perfectness.

That is not possible.

The midwife's lie was this: the bleeding never stops.

"Demons," say the Holy Men,

not worth their manly Hebrew time,

their wisdom weak against my love.

But this God of whom they speak—

defender of the orphan, comforter of widows, light to nations,

slow to anger, swift to heal—this One made Old Sarah laugh.

By such a One it surely is not possible my love will go unheard.

And now and here, my godforsaken corner of the world,

He comes, the One, the Son, they say,

of this One God who won't shrug off

a mongrel bitch who comes in trust and love.

Meek and humble he's supposed to be,

and yet like all the rest a posse closes ranks.

Though on my native turf, I am a foreigner to them.
This is not possible.

And so beneath their waving, kosher arms
I'm not too proud to bow and speak to him.
His voice is gentle but the words demean.
This is not possible.

More possible that I should shrug my dignity
than that this Son should withhold mercy
and so I bow again, will bow until
the sun shall bleed away and be no more.

It is not possible that love should be refused.
He calls this faith, but all I know is love.

People who have visited the Holy Land report how meaningful it is to follow in Jesus' footsteps: wading in the Jordan River, walking beside the Sea of Galilee, treading the Via Dolorosa where Jesus carried his cross to his death. But even if you never visit the Holy Land, you can still walk with Jesus in your imagination.

When I was a little girl, I had an active imagination and was often told that I "let my imagination run away with me." From this I developed a bit of guilt about using my imagination and concluded that imagination certainly does not belong in prayer, where it is important to be pious and serious with God. If you carry this kind of baggage, kindly throw it out.

Imaginative prayer opens doors in your relationship with God that cannot be penetrated by the rational mind. In the weeks that follow, you will read lots of stories about Jesus. Some will be so familiar that you may assume you already "know" them as well as they can be known. However, entering into the stories as an active participant through the imagination allows a deeper knowledge, a heart-knowledge, a potentially transformative knowledge. If in the past you have known *about* Jesus, imaginative prayer allows you to know *him* as a companion in your journey.

I wrote the poem on the preceding page after a session of imaginative prayer with Matthew 15:21-28. I drew upon my own experience as a mother to identify with the mother in the story. "Not Possible" begins as a protest (not possible that her child isn't perfect, not possible that foreigners should treat her as the alien on her home turf, not possible that the Son of God should refuse her request) and ends up being an avowal of faith: It is not possible that love should not prevail. I ended up wondering if Jesus the man may have needed this woman's witness to the triumph of love in order to be able to face his Passion later on.

Your imaginative prayer will most likely not take you to the same place mine took me. The value in imaginative prayer is that it reveals what you in particular need to see, drawing upon your own memories and the associations that make sense to you.

As you journal through this section, here are some questions that may be helpful: What does your imaginative reading of this passage tell you about God? How does this clarify your vision of Jesus? How can you identify with Jesus or with his teaching in this passage? What does this tell you about following Jesus? Imagine having a conversation with Jesus in which you share your answers to any of these questions. Hear his response.

Before we begin this adventure with Jesus, let us think about why we follow him. What authority has he over us? Why do we respond to his call? How do we respond to his call?

PRAYER EXERCISES

- Dispose yourself for prayer.

- Breathe deeply, at least one cleansing breath.

- Pray for the grace of the week.

- Read through the entire day's prompt before beginning the first step.

- Practice *lectio divina* with the scripture passages.

- Journal your answers to each day's prayer prompts, or otherwise as you are moved.

- Offer your reflections to God in prayer.

- Do not forget to do your daily examen sometime before bed.

WEEK 7

THE CALL GOES OUT

This week, the *grace* is:

To hear and be ready to respond to Christ's invitation to join him in God's work.

DAY 1: THE INVITATION OF A RIGHTEOUS LEADER

Scripture: Luke 4:16-19; Luke 7:20-22

Imagine a leader with an infectious vision of peace, justice, and healing. The person has a credible plan to bring about this vision and recruits you to join in. The leader promises that it will be very hard work, but that there is no hardship that the person will not share, working shoulder-to-shoulder with you. You will be provided with everything you need to do your part. As you will have shared in the work, you will also share in the ultimate victory.

Do not worry about how unlikely this is in the "real world." For the purposes of this exercise, you are not in the real world, but in the realm of your imagination. Fix the picture of the righteous leader in your mind. How do you respond to this person?

DAY 2: "FOLLOW ME"

Scripture: Matthew 4:17-22; Matthew 16:24-25

Yesterday you imagined your response to a worldly invitation to work viably for justice, peace, and healing in the world under the leadership and in the companionship of a righteous and generous person, knowing that the work would be hard but the eventual reward very great. The parallel is obvious to Jesus and his invitation to you to share his work.

Jesus' work is nothing less than the healing of the whole world. It is a huge endeavor, and Jesus enlists your help, vowing that as you share the hardships of his work, you will also share his companionship and his ultimate glory. Here is the thing: No one emerges from this work unchanged. Yet the rewards are beyond imagining.

How ready are you to respond to Christ's call? What, if anything, makes you hesitate? Please understand that, for many, responding to the call to follow Jesus is a process that begins tentatively and grows gradually. Where are you in this process?

DAY 3: RADICAL COMMITMENT

Scripture: Matthew 19:27-30; John 6:66-69

The disciples clearly made a radical commitment to following Jesus Christ. Ignatius expressed his own aspiration to their level of commitment in the following prayer:

Eternal Lord and King of all creation, humbly I come before you. Knowing the support of Mary, your mother, and all your saints, I am moved by your grace to offer myself to you and to your work. I deeply desire to be with you in accepting all wrongs and all abuse and all poverty, both actual and spiritual – and I deliberately choose this, if it is for your greater service and praise. If you, my Lord and King, would so call and choose me, then take and receive me into such a way of life. (SE 98)[21]

---

[21] Fleming, *Exercises*, 67.

Ignatius is not a masochist. He does not arbitrarily choose abuse and poverty, but volunteers himself to God's service, whatever God intends for him, even to the point of abuse and poverty if need be, as Jesus volunteered himself.

This prayer is known as "The Prayer for Generosity." What feelings does it arouse in you? Can you imagine being able to pray this prayer from your own heart?

We will return to this prayer later in these exercises to see how your feelings about it evolve.

DAY 4: SETTING THE SCENE

Scripture: John 1:1-5

> First [I see] those on the face of the earth, in such great diversity in dress and in manner of acting. Some are white, some black; some at peace, and some at war; some weeping, some laughing; some well, some sick; some coming into the world and some dying.
>
> Secondly, I will see and consider the Three Divine Persons seated on the royal dais or throne of the Divine Majesty. They look down upon the whole surface of the earth, and behold all nations in great blindness... (SE 106)[22]

As mentioned in Week 1, for many of his meditations, Ignatius invites consideration of the "place" and the "grace." Every week so far, we have had a grace to consider. Now, to introduce the Incarnation, Ignatius

---

[22] Ignatius, *Exercises*, 41-42.

specifically asks us to envision the place, to set the scene for everything that is to follow. In this case, the place is nothing less than planet Earth.

Imagine you have the power to scan the earth from a great vantage, observing the vast human family in all its variety, going about its business, oblivious, for the most part, to its place in history and creation. What feelings does this arouse in you? What is it to be human? What feelings arise when you think of God caring for this mass of humanity?

DAY 5: THE HOLY TRINITY

This will be to listen to what the persons on the face of the earth say, that is, how they speak to one another, swear and blaspheme, etc. I will also hear what the Divine Persons say, that is, "Let us work the redemption of the human race..." (SE 107).[23]

The leap of divine joy: God knows that the time has come when the mystery of his salvific plan, hidden from the beginning of the world, will become manifest. (SE 108).[24]

God, in all Three Persons, is eternal. But God chose a specific moment in time to send the Son into the world in fulfillment of God's plan. What do you feel when you contemplate the moment at which the great work of the Incarnation was set in motion?

---

[23] Ignatius, *Exercises*, 42.

[24] Fleming, *Exercises*, 73.

DAY 6: COLLOQUY

Scripture: John 1:14-18

> *I will think over what I ought to say to the Three Divine*
> *Persons, or to the eternal Word incarnate, or to His Mother,*
> *our Lady. According to the light that I have received, I will beg*
> *for grace to follow and imitate more closely our Lord, who has*
> *just become man for me.* (SE 109)[25]

As described in the previous chapter, what Ignatius calls a "colloquy" is an imagined conversation with God, in any of the three Persons of the Godhead, or with the Virgin Mary.

Have a colloquy with the Father, Son, Holy Spirit, or Mother Mary in which you describe what the Incarnation means to you. Hear God's response. Write a prayer of thanksgiving and ask for the grace to follow Jesus wholeheartedly.

DAY 7: REPETITION

Review the last week, rereading your journal entries. What in the prayer prompts, scripture readings, or the Ignatian citations stands out for you? What made the deepest impression? What are your thoughts and feelings about the Incarnation at this point? Return to the places of deepest grace that you experienced this week. Are you moved to go deeper? How? Thank God for any graces received this week.

---

[25] Ignatius, *Exercises*, 42.

WEEK 8

THE GREAT WORK BEGINS

This week, the *grace* is:

To know wonder and joy at the miracle of the Incarnation.

DAY 1: GABRIEL

Scripture: Luke 1:26-38

A few weeks ago we talked about angels. Whatever else angels are, according to the Bible they are messengers from God. How does God communicate with you? Have you ever felt that God was communicating with you through the voice of another person? What was that like, and what gave you the feeling the message was godly?

Have you ever brought a godly message to another? Before you answer, ponder whether teaching a child to pray, visiting a sick person, or some similar act of compassion can be considered bringing a godly message.

DAY 2: MARY

Scripture: Luke 1:26-38

Imagine the place. Traditional depictions of the Annunciation show Mary in her home, but if you can imagine this scene better in the open air, go with your heart. You can observe as a bystander, or you can take the part of Gabriel or of Mary. What do you see, smell, taste, hear, feel? What emotions arise? What brings Mary to that momentous statement, "Here am I, the servant of the Lord; let it be with me according to your word"? Can you conceive of saying those words in your own voice?

How has your perception of Mary evolved as a result of this exercise?

DAY 3: MAGNIFICAT

Scripture: Luke 1:39-55

Imagine the place. The trip from Nazareth to the hill country of Judea was a journey of some days on foot. What is Mary's motivation to visit her relative Elizabeth so far away? What are her feelings along the way? Take the part of an observer, or of Elizabeth or Mary as they meet and embrace. Experience the bond between the two miraculously pregnant women.

Speak Mary's words aloud. Can you identify an experience where, like Mary, you felt profoundly blessed by God?

The scripture tells us Mary remained with Elizabeth for three months. This suggests she stayed with Elizabeth through the remainder of Elizabeth's pregnancy. What do you think they did together and spoke about during that time?

What have you learned about Mary and Elizabeth?

DAY 4: JOSEPH

Scripture: Matthew 1:18-25

Picture the place. Joseph hears that Mary is pregnant and knows he is not the father. What might be his feelings? By law, Mary could be stoned to death! How does he reach his decision to dissolve the engagement "quietly"?

Now imagine his dream and his awakening. What changes have taken place in his heart and mind? Can you put yourself in his place? What are your feelings?

What have you learned about Joseph?

Angels are always telling people not to be afraid. What if, today, angels told you not to be afraid? What would they be talking about in your case?

DAY 5: JOURNEY TO BETHLEHEM

Scripture: Luke 2:3-5

Mary, heavily pregnant, sets out with Joseph for Bethlehem. Ignatius suggests they are accompanied by a maidservant. Why not? If you like, imagine being the maid. What do you observe along this journey? What do you feel for Mary and Joseph?

Imagine the place: "Consider its length, its breadth; whether level, or through valleys and over hills" (SE 112).[26] Nazareth to Bethlehem is about 70 miles. This is most likely a challenging trip. Might there be consolations as well?

How does your faith journey compare with this physical journey undertaken by Mary and Joseph?

DAY 6: NATIVITY

Scripture: Luke 2:6-7

So much of the mythology surrounding the Nativity comes down to these two short verses. Know that in imagining this part of Jesus' story you do not need to be bound by conventional representations of Christmas. Imagine the place: "whether big or little; whether high or low; and how it

---

[26] Ignatius, *Exercises*, 43.

is arranged" (SE 112).[27] Imagine you are present. You can be the maid again, or possibly a midwife who has been summoned. What is it like being present at the labor and birth? Observe Mary and Joseph in their first moments of parenthood. Are you moved to help and serve them? How?

Gaze on the infant Jesus. Does he have that wonderful new baby smell? Touch his hand, or even, at Mary's invitation, hold him in your arms. What feelings arise in you? What can it possibly mean that this helpless baby is the Almighty God incarnate?

What have you learned about Jesus' humanity?

DAY 7: REPETITION

Review the last week, rereading your journal entries. What in the prayer prompts, Scripture readings, or the Ignatian citations stands out for you? What made the deepest impression? What have you learned about angels, Mary, Elizabeth, Joseph, and Jesus? What have you learned about yourself? What does the Incarnation mean to you now? Thank God for any graces received this week.

---

[27] Ignatius, *Exercises*, 43.

WEEK 9

THE FIRST WORSHIPERS

This week, the *grace* is:

To adore the infant Jesus.

DAY 1: SHEPHERDS IN THE FIELD

Scripture: Luke 2:8-14

Imagine the place: the fields in the hills around Bethlehem at night. You are a humble shepherd surrounded by your flock. What do you see, smell, taste, hear, feel? The angel appears. How?

Experience the range of emotions attributed to the shepherds in the scripture. What do you hear in the angel's words? What in the world is a multitude of the heavenly host? What does their praise sound like? Have you ever, in your own real-life experience, heard anything that might be comparable?

DAY 2: SHEPHERDS IN THE STABLE

Scripture: Luke 2:15-20

Imagine the shepherds' excited conversation. Is the decision to go to Bethlehem unanimous? How do you feel about it? What is the journey into town like? How do you know where to go? Finally, you find Mary and Joseph and Jesus. Again, what do you see, smell, taste, hear and feel?

What is the return like? How do you "make known" what you have experienced? In the voice of a shepherd, write in your journal how you would express what you have seen and heard this night. What words would a shepherd use to glorify and praise God?

DAY 3: WISE MEN

Scripture: Matthew 2:1-12

As yesterday you put yourself in the place of a shepherd, now imagine being an eastern sage, or one of his or her retinue. Picture the sighting of the star, the long voyage, the audience with Herod, and then the arrival at the Holy Family's house. Again, what do you see, smell, taste, hear and feel? Converse with Mary and Joseph. Touch or even hold the baby. Offer your gifts and register the way they are received.

What gifts would you have offered as a wise man? What gifts do you offer today, as yourself? What has been your guiding star in life?

DAY 4: PRESENTATION

Scripture: Luke 2:22-24

Luke's narrative seems to combine two Jewish rituals: purification after childbirth and dedication of a firstborn male child. To modern sensibilities, it may offend that a woman would need to be purified after childbirth, but bear in mind the ritual may also have provided an opportunity for the woman to give thanks for a healthy delivery, the perils of childbirth being as high as they were. If you were Mary, what would you be feeling as you go to Jerusalem to make the required offering?

Imagine the place: the Temple in Jerusalem, the most holy site in the world for Jews, the very dwelling place of the Most High. Think of Mary and Joseph ascending the steps and crossing the threshold. What might be in their hearts? What are they expecting?

Luke's narrative suggests that fulfilling religious obligations was important to Joseph and Mary. In your life, how do rituals express your faith and devotion to God?

DAY 5: SIMEON

Scripture: Luke 2:25-35

Picture Simeon. How did the Holy Spirit reveal to him that he would see the Messiah? Imagine him hurrying to the Temple, seeing the Holy Family, taking Jesus in his arms, and breaking into song. Read his words aloud and try to feel his joy. Now imagine what this sounded and looked like to Joseph and Mary.

Have you ever, like Simeon, had something come true that you had hoped for a long time? Even if you offered thanks to God at the time, relive the experience and offer thanks anew. Then offer any gratitude you feel for the gift of Jesus.

DAY 6: ANNA

Scripture: Luke 2:36-38

Female characters in the Bible are not always identified by name. Anna is an exception. As a widow of many years' standing, she probably had not had an easy life. At 84, she was exceptionally old for that time and place. Imagine her frequenting the Temple. Did most people view her as a sage or as a crazy old lady, do you suppose?

Unlike Simeon, Anna is not quoted in the Bible. In her place, what would you have said?

Why do you think people who have a prophetic voice are sometimes regarded as crazy?

DAY 7: REPETITION

Review the last week, rereading your journal entries. What in the prayer prompts or scripture readings stands out for you? What made the deepest impression? What have you learned about the people who first recognized the baby Jesus as the Messiah? Can you identify with them? What signs help you recognize the presence of Christ? Thank God for any graces received this week.

WEEK 10

THE "HIDDEN YEARS"

This week, the *grace* is:

To mature and grow in the Lord, in imitation of the youthful Jesus.

DAY 1: REFUGEES

Scripture: Matthew 2:13-18

Consider the similarities between this part of Jesus' story and the story of Moses: the ruler, jealous of his own power, ordering the massacre of babies and children; and the Egyptian exile.

Nothing is more tragic in human history, then and now, than when the innocent suffer for the sins of the powerful. Ponder how this phenomenon will be echoed in Jesus' own eventual death. Pray for God's mercy on our race. Pray for the refugees of our own day and ask for guidance in serving them in Jesus' name.

DAY 2: NAZARETH

Scripture: Matthew 2:19-23

Matthew implies that the Holy Family's settling in Nazareth in Galilee was a second choice, based on fear of the Herodians still in power in Jerusalem. This accident of fate resulted in a prophecy being fulfilled, which later helped to validate Jesus' claim to be the Messiah. Have you ever experienced such an "accident" that seemed, in retrospect, to be fortuitous? Have you ever experienced a coincidence that on reflection afterwards seemed to indicate the hand of God? Do you believe God works in our lives in ways of which we may be unconscious at the time? Why or why not?

DAY 3: THE YOUNG JESUS

Scripture: Luke 2:39-40

The Bible provides no information about most of Jesus' childhood and young adulthood. For this reason, this period of Jesus' life is referred to as the "Hidden Years." The value in imagining this period is in drawing ever closer to Jesus, knowing him better and better to facilitate following him more and more closely. Imagine Jesus at the ages of 2, 5, 8, and 10 years. Picture Jesus' religious training, his going to the synagogue with his parents, playing, and working alongside Joseph. It may help to remember yourself or your children at those ages. At what ages did you become aware of your own particular gifts or interests? How might Jesus' self-awareness have developed? What feelings arise when you think of Jesus as a child like yourself or like your own children? Express your feelings to God in prayer.

DAY 4: HIS FATHER'S HOUSE

Scripture: Luke 2:41-50

Picture the trip to Jerusalem, on foot in a large group of friends and relatives; the confusion, the camaraderie, the fatigue, the expectation, the arrival, and the festivities. Jesus must have been in the habit of spending a lot of time with trusted companions for Mary and Joseph to begin the return trip without their being concerned about him. Imagine their increasingly frantic feelings as they search everywhere along the way before arriving back in Jerusalem. Let the scene play out in your mind. Try taking the part of different characters: Mary, Joseph, the teachers, Jesus himself. What are you learning about Jesus?

DAY 5: COLLOQUY WITH MARY

Scripture: Luke 2:51

So far in our story, Mary has had to absorb experiences that would have tried the faith and sanity of a woman several times her age. Consider the kinds of announcements that have fallen on her young ears:

- "You will conceive and bear a son...the Holy Spirit will come upon you."
- "The mother of my Lord comes to me."
- The shepherd's testimony.
- The wise men's adoration.
- "A sword will piece your own soul too."
- "Did you not know I must be in my Father's house?"

Mary has had a lot to "treasure in her heart." Imagine a conversation with her in which you ask her what all this was like for her. How do you respond to what she says?

DAY 6: JESUS AS A YOUNG MAN

Scripture: Luke 2:52

Just as you imagined Jesus as a child a few days ago, now imagine his growing up: Jesus at 15, 20, and 25; studying, learning a trade, working alongside his father, assuming more and more responsibility. We are told he grew wise and was well regarded. What joys and sorrows might he have known? How aware is he of his vocation? Imagine meeting him at this age. What would you talk about?

Pray that you may follow his example, increasing in wisdom as your own years increase.

DAY 7: REPETITION

Review the last week, rereading your journal entries. What in the prayer prompts or Scripture readings stands out for you? What made the deepest impression? What have you learned about Jesus the man? Are you able to identify with him any more closely? Thank God for any graces received this week.

WEEK 11

ASSIMILATION AND TRANSITION

This week, the *grace* is:

To identify with the young Jesus in preparation for accompanying him into his active ministry

DAY 1: THE AGE OF SURROUNDING LOVE

Scripture: Matthew 2:10-11

We are about to begin the great adventure of joining Jesus in his earthly ministry. As we transition into this phase, let us pause to relate personally to Jesus' early life. We do this to develop a habit of identifying with Jesus as we are able, that we may follow him more closely in our own lives.

Jesus was adored as a newborn baby. Indeed, most newborn babies are adored, or ought to be. The fortunate among us can remember an early childhood where love surrounded us to the extent that we took that love for granted, only later having to learn that not everybody was going to love us. If you can remember a time when you were so surrounded by love that you never questioned it, go there now in your memory. If you cannot, try to imagine what it is like to be so surrounded by unquestioned and adoring love. Spend several moments considering that this is the kind of love God has for you. You are God's much-wanted and treasured child.

DAY 2: THE AGE OF OBEDIENCE

Scripture: Luke 2:51

We are told that as a child Jesus was obedient to his parents. As an adult he was obedient to God. What is your experience with obedience?

Obedience generally means something different to an adult than to a child. It may mean something different to a woman than to a man. What does it mean to you? To whom or to what do you give obedience? How is being obedient to God like and unlike being obedient to humans or human institutions?

DAY 3: THE AGE OF DISCERNMENT

Scripture: Luke 2:52

According to scripture Jesus set out to fulfill his earthly ministry when he was about 30 years old. Last week we considered what he might have been doing as a young adult up to that point. Most of us discern our earthly vocation as young adults, and presumably Jesus did too. How did you go about discerning what you would do professionally as a young adult? Did you go through subsequent discernments later in life, as for example, whether to get married, have children, move, or change jobs? Was God's calling to you a part of those discernments? What does discernment mean to you at your current stage of life? Are there particular issues that you want to bring before God now?

Several weeks from now, toward the end of these exercises, we will return to the subject of where God might be calling you at this point in your life. For now, simply consider that God continues to call us throughout our lives. As your life evolves, so does your baptismal vocation.

DAY 4: THE TWO STANDARDS

> *Here it will be that Christ calls and wants all beneath His standard, and Lucifer, on the other hand, wants all under his. (SE 137)*[28]

Ignatius the soldier conceived the cosmic struggle between good and evil as a battlefield across which the armies of Christ and of Lucifer face each other. It is not necessary to adopt a militaristic metaphor to consider that following Jesus is frequently complicated if not downright thwarted by prevailing cultural forces. In your journal, on one page list some standards by which the world operates, such as, "Look out for number one." On another page, list the standards for which Christ stands, such as, "Love your neighbor." To which of the items on your first list are you most susceptible? Which of the items on your second list do you find easiest? Which are most difficult? Pray for the grace to follow Christ more closely.

DAY 5: THREE TYPES

> *They all wish to save their souls and find peace in God our Lord by ridding themselves of the burden arising from the attachment ... which impedes the attainment of this end. (SE 150)*[29]

Ignatius presents an analogy of three types of people who want to be faithful to God by disposing virtuously of some ill-gotten gains. The first type has good intensions but never gets around to doing anything. The second truly wants the peace that will come with divestment but also wants

---

[28] Ignatius, *Exercises*, 48.

[29] Ignatius, *Exercises*, 50.

to retain some benefit from the property. The third wants only to please God and is indifferent to whether he keeps the property or gives it away. This third type is willing to do whichever serves God's purpose.

Where do you see yourself in this story? Most of us find ourselves somewhere in the middle. What do you most treasure? Make a list of the things in your life you would find hardest to do without. Review the list and consider the extent to which each item may serve God.

DAY 6: ENCOURAGEMENT

When we are trying to follow the call of the Lord in our life, we will find that the good spirit tends to give support, encouragement, and oftentimes even a certain delight in all our endeavors.

The evil spirit generally acts to bring about the opposite reaction. The evil spirit will subtly arouse a dissatisfaction with our own efforts, will raise up doubts and anxieties about God's love or our own response, or sting the conscience with thoughts of pride in our attempt to lead a good life. (SE 329)[30]

Scripture: John 16:33

You are now almost a third of the way through these exercises. How are you doing? By now you will probably have developed some kind of pattern in your prayer life. What is working for you? What is difficult?

Ignatius in his wisdom recognized that at this point in the exercises some people begin to doubt themselves and wonder whether they are cut

---

[30] Fleming, *Exercises*, 215.

out for this kind of work. Be sure to bring this type of misgiving into your sessions with your spiritual director. In many cases, discouragement at this stage is evidence of the false self resisting self-examination and growth. Call upon God for strength, and be confident in God's help. It is God's work you are about, after all. As Jesus says in the King James Version of the Bible: "Be of good cheer! I have overcome the world!"

Continue to monitor your consolations and desolations.

DAY 7: REPETITION

Review the last week, rereading your journal entries. What in the prayer prompts, scripture readings, or Ignatian quotations stands out for you? What made the deepest impression?

In what ways have you identified with the young Jesus? What have you learned about yourself? Thank God for any graces received this week.

WEEK 12

BAPTISM AND TEMPTATION

This week, the *grace* is:

To see Jesus during his baptism and temptation in order to know him more intimately, love him more completely and follow him more closely.

DAY 1: JOHN AND JESUS

Scripture: Mark 1:6-8; John 1:24-34

What do you think the relationship between John the Baptist and Jesus was like? We know that because their mothers were related, they may have known *about* each other, but because Jesus grew up in Nazareth and John's family lived in Judea, it is possible they never met until Jesus came to be baptized. But John seems to have faith and hope in Jesus before he even saw him. How do you think he acquired that faith and hope? How did you acquire *your* faith and hope in Jesus?

How do you think John perceived his own vocation? In what ways is your vocation as a Christian like that of John's? John recognized Jesus immediately. How would you recognize Jesus if you saw him?

DAY 2: BAPTISM

Scripture: Matthew 3:1-17

Imagine the place: the banks of the Jordan River near Jerusalem. Imagine John in his peculiar mode of dress, and the people coming out to hear him preach, to be baptized, or to question him. How do you feel when you hear him speak of judgment and "unquenchable fire"? What do you think attracts people to him?

Now imagine Jesus arriving. Hear the conversation between John and Jesus. Observe Jesus' baptism. Do you perceive the descent of the Holy Spirit "like a dove," or is that something Jesus and John alone experience? What is the "voice from heaven" like? What feelings arise in you as you contemplate this scene?

DAY 3: FASTING AND WILDERNESS

Scripture: Luke 4:1-2; Mark 1:12-13

Wilderness is a powerful metaphor with strong meaning for the Jews because of their ancestors' sojourn in the wilderness as they awaited entrance into the Promised Land. What does wilderness mean to you? What "wildernesses" have you experienced in your life?

Have you ever fasted? If so, how and why were you moved to do it? What was your experience with it? What are the reasons for fasting? If you feel called, and only if your health allows, consider a fast of 24 hours to experience something of what Jesus knew. You may want to try to fast from something other than food, like fasting from watching TV or from using your phone or computer. If you decide to fast, fix in your mind why you are doing it. What do you expect from your fast?

DAY 4: TEMPTED TO TAKE THE EASY WAY OUT

Scripture: Matthew 4:1-4; Luke 4:3-4

If you have fasted during the last day, what was that like? Did your fast accomplish what you expected it to?

Imagine the place: the wilderness. Imagine Jesus' loneliness and hunger as he comes to the end of his fast. What is the temptation to make bread from stones all about? Is it just about food, or something else? What do you think might have happened if Jesus had used his power to create food for himself at this point in his ministry?

To identify with Jesus in this temptation, you don't have to have experienced starvation. Try to think of a time you experienced great need or pain. If someone had said, "Just snap your fingers and I can make this all go away," what would you have done? Would you have accepted without considering unforeseen consequences? Would you have taken into account what that person's motives might have been and the possible cost to you and to others?

By resisting this temptation, what did Jesus accomplish? What does this exercise tell you about Jesus? What does it tell you about your own temptations?

DAY 5: TEMPTED TO IMPRESS PEOPLE
Scripture: Matthew 4:5-7; Luke 4:9-12

We are still in the wilderness. Imagine Jesus contemplating the work ahead of him. How aware is he of the frustrations, hardships, and trials he will have to endure? What do you think might have happened if Jesus had done this ostentatious thing to demonstrate his superhuman powers?

To identify with Jesus in this temptation, imagine that someone offered you a painless and instant way to accomplish all your life goals. You can have that advanced degree without the years of study. You can rise to the top of your profession without any work or sacrifice. What then? Even if you are at a stage of life where this kind of deal no longer attracts you, you can probably imagine how tempting the offer would be to a young person just starting out. Even now, you may feel the occasional temptation to take short cuts.

Mother Teresa is supposed to have said, "We can do no great things, only small things with great love." How does this quotation relate to Jesus' temptation to do something spectacular?

DAY 6: TEMPTED BY EARTHLY GLORY

Scripture: Matthew 4:8-11; Luke 4:5-8

Yes, still in the wilderness. That's the problem with wilderness: It seems to go on so long, and often you can't see the way out.

The devil tempts Jesus with earthly power. But if we read this passage closely, political power is not the only thing the devil offers. Matthew speaks of "splendor," and Luke mentions "glory and authority." In addition to power, the devil offers wealth, reputation, and influence. What might Jesus have been able to accomplish with all these advantages?

What kind of power have you ever wished for? The power to attract, to please, to persuade? What if someone promised you that, in return for your allegiance to him, you would never again be unrecognized or unappreciated? Use your feelings as you contemplate this scenario to try to identify with Jesus in this last temptation.

DAY 7: REPETITION

Review the last week, rereading your journal entries. What made the deepest impression? In what ways have you identified with Jesus in his baptism and temptation? What have you learned about yourself?

Have a colloquy with Jesus, asking him how he decided when to exercise his superhuman powers. Express your understanding and/or appreciation for what he accomplished in his temptation.

WEEK 13

JESUS' MINISTRY BEGINS

This week, the *grace* is:

To hear and respond to Jesus' call to discipleship

DAY 1: "COME AND SEE"

Scripture: John 1:35-51

Imagine the place: Presumably we are at the Jordan River with John when Jesus comes along. Pretend you are there, either observing or taking the part of one of the characters. Let the scene play out as described. Attend to how the various disciples come to follow Jesus. Andrew comes to Jesus on John's testimony. Simon Peter comes to Jesus on Andrew's testimony. Jesus personally invites Philip, and Philip invites Nathanael, who comes skeptically at first.

How did you come to Jesus? Was it because of a teacher (like Andrew) or a relative (like Simon Peter) or a friend (like Nathanael) or because you perceived an invitation from Jesus himself? Were you skeptical at first? If so, what won you over? Or are there parts of you that are still skeptical?

Say a prayer of thanksgiving for the people who introduced you to Jesus, or helped you know him better.

DAY 2: "FOLLOW ME"

Scripture: Matthew 4:18-22; Mark 1:16-20

Matthew and Mark tell a somewhat different story of how Simon Peter and Andrew came to follow Jesus. Here the place is the Sea of Galilee. Picture the fishing vessels and the men in them tending to their nets after a night spent fishing. Smell the fish. Hear Jesus' appeal.

What was there about these men that led Jesus to call them? What was there about Jesus that immediately appealed to these men? James and John left not only their boat but also their father. What were they feeling? What was their father Zebedee feeling? Have you ever had an experience of leaving something you cared about to do something you felt you had to do? What was it that compelled or enabled you to do that?

Pray for the strength always to respond positively to Jesus' invitation to follow him.

DAY 3: "DO NOT BE AFRAID"

Scripture: Luke 5:1-11

Luke here gives a more detailed story about the calling of Simon Peter than we have read so far. Imagine the place: the seaside where the fishermen are repairing their nets after a night of fishing. Jesus arrives with a group of followers. Do the see-smell-taste-hear-feel inventory. Play out the scene in your imagination, taking the part of Simon Peter. What's your reaction when Jesus plops himself into your boat? How do feel listening to his teaching? How do you react when he asks you to take your boat out again after hours of discouraging work (fishermen worked at night)? What makes you react to the miraculous catch with fear and make you think of your sinfulness? How do you then transition into wanting to follow Jesus?

Have you ever, like Simon Peter, felt unworthy to be Jesus' disciple?

DAY 4: "NOT THE RIGHTEOUS BUT THE SINNERS"

Scripture: Matthew 9:9-13

Here Jesus calls someone into discipleship who is not a fisherman. For pious Jews like the Pharisees, "tax collectors and sinners" was a redundancy. Tax collectors were collaborators and cheats. Yet this tax collector also followed Jesus immediately.

Picture the place: a public place in Galilee. Take the part of Matthew and imagine the scene. What goes on in your mind and heart when Jesus calls you? What inspires you to invite Jesus and his disciples to dinner with all your tax collector colleagues? What do you expect from this dinner? What do you hear when Jesus says, "I have come not to call the righteous, but sinners"?

What does this exercise tell you about following Jesus? How adequately does it address any feelings of unworthiness for you?

DAY 5: THE WEDDING AT CANA

Scripture: John 2:1-11

Imagine this wedding. Wedding celebrations in Jesus' day could go on for several days. Apparently to run out of wine was something of a scandal for the hosts.

First, imagine you are Mary. Why do you approach your son about the wine crisis? How do you interpret his assertion that his "time has not yet come"? Now put yourself in Jesus' place. What makes you demur when your mother first appeals to you? What then happens in your heart and mind that you decide to act? Finally, pretend to be one of the servants.

What is your reaction when you see that the water has turned to wine?

What makes you believe in Jesus? What reveals his glory to you?

DAY 6: CLEANSING THE TEMPLE

Scripture: John 2:13-22

Here we are in Jerusalem again at the temple. Play the scene out in your imagination, taking the part of a bystander. Do your see-smell-taste-hear-feel inventory. How do you react? Hear Jesus' pronouncement about raising up the temple in three days. What does that mean to you?

John places this scene at the very beginning of Jesus' public ministry, while the other Gospels place it just before the Passion, and we will revisit it in a few weeks. Do not be overly concerned about this apparent discrepancy, but try to see what truth John is communicating by putting this story first. Why would Jesus begin his career this way?

DAY 7: REPETITION

Review the last week, rereading your journal entries. How is Jesus' call to you like and unlike his calls to the first disciples? How does the miracle at Cana and the cleansing of the temple prepare you for following Jesus through the coming exercises? What feelings do you have about what lies ahead?

Thank God for any graces received this week.

WEEK 14

JESUS THE TEACHER

We are going to spend the next week with the Sermon on the Mount, which, according to Matthew's Gospel, Jesus preached early in his ministry. Imagining the place for a teaching passage can be a bit challenging. You can, of course, imagine yourself on the mountain, listening to Jesus preach and observing the effects upon yourself as part of his first-century audience. But a more effective approach may be to register the effects upon yourself in your current situation. The place in this instance is less a physical setting than a mental, spiritual, and emotional state. Imagine Jesus speaking directly to you and take note of how you feel listening to his words and how you might respond.

This week, the *grace* is:

To hear and respond to Jesus' teaching and preaching.

DAY 1: THE BEATITUDES

Scripture: Matthew 5:1-11

In Jesus' day, people often believed that happiness and prosperity were signs of God's favor. Though now we naturally find this quaint idea overly simplistic, it persists today even among sophisticated people when they are stressed. Several times, people experiencing misfortune have asked me, "Why does God hate me?" Have you ever been tempted to think this way?

In the Beatitudes, Jesus plainly says that people who are spiritually impoverished, grieving, meek, or persecuted are blessed. He is turning conventional wisdom on its ear. Think of the low points of your own life. In what way could they be considered blessings? If so, could you bring yourself to thank God for them? What words would you use to do this?

DAY 2: SALT AND LIGHT

Scripture: Matthew 5:13-16

What does it mean to be salt of the earth and light of the world? What taste do you leave in the mouths of people with whom you deal? In what ways do you let your light shine before others? In what ways do you hide your light under a bushel basket? If people were to judge what your God is like on the basis of your words and actions, what would they think of God? Pray to be able to let God's light shine through you.

DAY 3: FULFILLMENT OF THE LAW

Scripture: Matthew 5:17-48

In this section, Jesus states that rather than superseding the Mosaic law, he has come to fulfill it. He then cites various provisions of the law, preaching an even higher standard than the law dictates. He puts anger, insult, and contempt on a par with murder and equates lust with adultery. Finally, he extends the law of love to enemies as well as neighbors. How do you react to these expectations? Does Jesus really expect people to meet standards this high? Have a colloquy privately with Jesus in which you ask him what he expects of you.

DAY 4: PRAYER

Scripture: Matthew 6:1-18

What relevance does Jesus' preaching on piety and prayer have to your own practice of piety and prayer? What are your expectations when you practice generosity in giving alms? Why pray if your Father knows what you need before you ask him?

Because we know the Lord's Prayer by heart, it is easy to rattle it off without thinking about it. Pray the Lord's prayer slowly and intentionally. Think of what each well-known phrase means to you personally. Then write your own version of the Lord's Prayer in your journal.

DAY 5: TREASURE

Scripture: Matthew 6:19-21

What do you seek, and when you find it, what do you hold close to yourself? What do you treasure? Make a list in your journal. What is lasting and what is not?

Have you ever had an experience of discovering that something you treasured was impermanent? Have you ever had an experience of pursuing something you thought you really wanted only to find it did not live up to expectations? Write about your feelings on these occasions. Pray to truly treasure your relationship with God.

DAY 6: WORRY

Scripture: Matthew 6:25-35

Are you a worrier? What kinds of things are apt to worry you? From what need in your life does that worry spring? If you are not a worrier, were you always this way? What, if anything, helps you stop worrying?

Make a list in your journal of any worries. Imagine bringing each one to Jesus and seeing him receive each one gently and respectfully, thanking you, and looking you in the eyes. Can you leave your worries with Jesus?

DAY 7: REPETITION

Review the last week, rereading your journal entries. What has stayed with you from Jesus' sermon? What in Jesus' teaching is easiest for you to receive, and what is most difficult? What has the most relevance to your life this week? What, if any, changes are you moved to make in your life as a result of having prayed with the Sermon on the Mount? How has your mental picture of Jesus grown or shifted as a result of carefully studying and praying this sermon?

Thank God for any graces received this week.

WEEK 15

PARABLES

From a week spent with Jesus' teaching in the Sermon on the Mount, we turn to another form of his teaching: the parables. Most of us know these stories so well, we often read them without thinking, without realizing the shock value they had when Jesus first told them. Try in the coming week to hear these familiar stories with new ears. It may help to imagine being part of Jesus' original audience, or to imagine going to church and hearing them preached from the pulpit today. Each of these stories has what one of my colleagues calls "a pinch and a promise." What is the pinch in each parable? What is the promise?

Try to summarize the truth that Jesus is trying to convey in each parable in your own words. Can you think of an example from your own experience that would express the same truth?

This week, the *grace* is:

To read, hear, mark, learn, and inwardly digest Jesus' teaching in the parables.

DAY 1: PARABLE OF THE SOWER

Scripture: Mark 4:1-9, 13-20

It's tempting to hear this story and immediately try to determine what kind of soil you are, and whether God's word is withering within you or bearing fruit. Instead of focusing on the soil and seed, focus on the sower. If you were sowing seed, would you sow as indiscriminately as the sower in the parable does? What does Jesus' parable say about God? If you were to ask the Father why he is so careless with the seed, what do you think he would say?

DAY 2: THE GOOD SAMARITAN

Scripture: Luke 10:29-37

Because Jesus concludes this parable by saying, "Go and do likewise," we assume that we are to model ourselves on the Samaritan. For a change, imagine yourself as the assault victim instead. Barely conscious, you are able to register each traveler passing by. What are your expectations of the priest, the Levite (a junior or senior warden might be a modern equivalent), and the Samaritan? Remember that Jews considered Samaritans apostates or heretics. If there are any so-called Christian groups that you believe don't really measure up to the name, they would represent a modern-day equivalent to the Samaritans. What is it like to be pitied and ministered to by a member of a group you have despised? What fruit can you draw from this exercise?

DAY 3: THE PRODIGAL SON

Scripture: Luke 15:11-32

Imagine it is the end of the day that the younger son has returned home, and everyone has retired to his room. By the light of an oil lamp, each of the three principals in this story, the younger son, the father, and the elder son, is writing in his diary. In your own journal, record in turn what each might say. Draw upon your own experiences to do this exercise. Which role is easiest for you to take? Why?

DAY 4: THE RICH MAN AND LAZARUS

Scripture: Luke 16:19-31

In a single phrase, write down in your journal what this parable is all about. Although the story is fanciful (can people in hell really negotiate with the patriarch Abraham on his heavenly perch?), what truth do you derive from it? What is the pinch for you? What is the promise?

DAY 5: THE UNJUST JUDGE

Scripture: Luke 18:1-8

What is your reaction to this parable? Do you find it disturbing that Jesus compares God to an impatient judge who grants a request just to get rid of an insistent petitioner? How does this story work for you in encouraging you to pray always and not lose heart?

Have you ever had a long-time prayer that never seemed to get answered? How did that feel? Were you tempted to lose heart? What happened? Was there anything in that instance that encouraged you to keep praying and not lose heart? What was it?

One of the most important aspects of prayer is always to be honest with God. Is there anything on your heart you hesitate to bring before God because it represents to you the "wrong" way to pray? If you are able, bring it now.

DAY 6: PARABLE OF THE TALENTS

Scripture: Matthew 25:14-30

A "talent" was a measure of weight applied to precious metals. A single talent, whether of gold or silver, represented a sum of immense value. Certainly verse 18 refers to the talent as "money." What do the talents in this parable represent to you? Obviously, a talent in this sense may not be anything material. With what of value have you been entrusted, and what have you done with it? You can certainly think of "talents" in the modern English sense of inborn aptitude or skill. What if your "talent" is instead the faith you have been given? What have you made of this faith in the course of your life?

DAY 7: REPETITION

Review the last week, rereading your journal entries. How has your mental picture of Jesus grown or shifted as a result of carefully studying and praying his parables? What have you learned about yourself and your relationship with God? Does your experience with these exercises suggest any changes in your life? If so, bring them before God and test them.

Thank God for any graces received this week.

WEEK 16

THE KINGDOM OF GOD

Many of the parables and much of Jesus' other teachings have to do with the kingdom of God, or to use the expression the Gospel-writer Matthew prefers, the kingdom of heaven.

Before we go on, a word about language: The word "kingdom" is an English translation of *basileia*, a feminine noun in the Greek. Many scholars and preachers prefer the neutral words "realm" or "reign" to avoid a sexist reference, but I have retained the traditional language for two reasons. First, that is the language still found in most translations of the Bible. But more importantly, in Jesus' mouth, the words "king" and "kingdom" become almost ironical. Jesus stands the whole idea of monarchy on its ear. He is not a king as others are. Jesus transforms kingship as he transforms the law, transforms worship, transforms the understanding of heaven. In this sense, the word "kingdom" is like the cross. Through Jesus, an instrument of torture became a symbol of salvation. What one associates with the cross has been totally transformed by Jesus. I believe Jesus redeems the word "kingdom" in the same way.[31]

As you go through this week, imagine hearing Jesus preach about the kingdom of God. Do you agree with all his examples? Feel free to question him in your imagination about the analogies he uses. Hear his replies.

This week, the *grace* is:

To hear and respond to Jesus' teaching and preaching about the kingdom of God.

---

[31] To emphasize the feminine dimension of God's reign, Matthew Fox in his book *Christian Mystics: 365 Readings and Meditations* (Novato, CA: New World Library, 2011) uses the expression "the queendom of God." Through this unexpected variation on "kingdom," Fox demonstrates Jesus' radicalization of the term.

DAY 1: WEEDS

Scripture: Matthew 13:24-30

How do you envision heaven? Many people think of heaven as a place of pure goodness to which righteous people go when they die. This parable is not entirely consistent with that vision. How does this parable inform your idea of heaven? What does this parable tell you about the world, and about God? What is the pinch, and what is the promise?

DAY 2: MUSTARD SEED AND LEAVEN

Scripture: Matthew 13:31-33

Here are two analogies about small beginnings that have significant consequences.

As we noted in Week 12 of these exercises, Mother Theresa is supposed to have said, "It is not possible to do great things, only small things with great love." Think of some small things done for you that meant a great deal to you and record them in your journal.

Have you ever done something small that had greater results than you expected? What does this tell you about the kingdom of God? What does this tell you about the significance of your own actions?

DAY 3: THE TREASURE IN THE FIELD AND THE PEARL OF GREAT VALUE

Scripture: Matthew 13:44-46

What is the treasure in your life? What is your pearl? What type of person would be able to make the kind of single-minded sacrifice made by the buyer of the field and the pearl merchant? Can you picture yourself as such a person? Can you picture God as such a person, willing to make such a sacrifice for you?

DAY 4: THE LOST SHEEP

Scripture: Matthew 18:12-14

No one puts 99 sheep at risk to go after one stray! Imagine being part of Jesus' original audience and hearing him preach this. Ask him for an explanation. What does he say?

Do you consider yourself one of the 99 or the one who needed rescue? How does your attitude toward the shepherd change depending on which role you take?

DAY 5: JESUS AND THE CHILDREN

Scripture: Matthew 19:13-15

Take the role of different characters in this story: a parent, a disciple, a child. Imagine being a child on whom Jesus lays his hands. What does that feel like? What is it like to come to Jesus as a child? In what ways are children the exemplars of people to whom the kingdom of heaven belongs? In what ways can you be like a child in the kingdom of heaven?

DAY 6: THE LABORERS

Scripture: Matthew 20:1-16

Once again, take the role of different characters in the story: the first laborers to arrive, who worked all day; then the latecomers. How does it feel that everyone is paid the same? What does this say about who deserves what? What do you feel you deserve?

What does this parable say about the kingdom of heaven? Do you think of yourself as a long-time laborer or a latecomer? Why? What does it mean to you that the last will be first and the first last?

DAY 7: REPETITION

Review the last week, rereading your journal entries. Why do you think Jesus spends so much time and energy preaching and teaching about the kingdom of God? What does this tell you about Jesus?

How has your understanding of heaven or the kingdom of God evolved? What have you learned about yourself and the way you live your life? How can you participate in the kingdom of heaven in the here and now? Does your experience with these exercises suggest any changes? If so, bring them before God and test them.

Thank God for any graces received this week.

WEEK 17

CONVERSATIONS

Much of what we know about Jesus as a person is from the conversations he had with people. This week, we will look at several of those encounters. In your imaginative prayer, take the part of his questioners. Try to identify with where they are coming from. Are you satisfied with Jesus' answers, or do you find that these answers simply raise more questions? Always pray your questions and never feel guilty about having them. Record them in your journal. Could it be that Jesus wants people to wrestle with their questions rather than be satisfied with a glib answer? How do you feel about that?

This week, the *grace* is:

To enter into conversation with Jesus, that you may know him more intimately, love him more dearly and follow him more closely.

DAY 1: NICODEMUS

Scripture: John 3:1-21

Nicodemus, a Pharisee, comes to Jesus by night. This early in John's Gospel, there does not seem to be much enmity between Jesus and the Pharisees, and yet there seems to be something surreptitious about this nighttime visit, as if Nicodemus wants to approach Jesus cautiously. Have you ever felt cautious in approaching Jesus? Why? What do you think Nicodemus is after?

What do you make of Jesus' answers to Nicodemus? What does it mean to you to be "born from above"? Jesus seems to be speaking in riddles. But then he comes out with that beloved and much-quoted verse, "For God so loved the world..." What does this verse mean to you? How does the remainder of this passage, in verses 17-21, elucidate for you what Jesus has said previously?

Make this exercise more than a purely intellectual process. Pause in your reflections to record how you feel encountering Jesus as Nicodemus did.

DAY 2: THE WOMAN AT THE WELL

Scripture: John 4:1-30, 39-42

Here we have an example of a woman whom the Gospel-writer does not name. To better identify with this person, give her a name.

Generations of (mostly male) interpreters have assumed that this woman must be a sinner if she has been married five times and now lives with a man out of wedlock. How likely is that in a time and place where women's rights and options were limited and marriages were arranged? How does your understanding of this story change if you imagine that what Jesus is acknowledging in his conversation with her is not that she has sinned but that she has been sinned against?

There are six exchanges between Jesus and the woman—an extraordinarily long conversation for the Bible! There is clearly some movement going on in the woman's consciousness. Take the part of the woman and register your feelings during each exchange with Jesus. Note these feelings in your journal, and try to identify with the woman's interior movement.

Consider whether people who have been sinned against need the liberation offered by Jesus as much as people who sin.

DAY 3: THE RICH YOUNG RULER

Scripture: Mark 10:17-22

Give this unidentified character a name too, to personalize him. Take his part. What is your motivation in coming to Jesus? Let the conversation play out. Feel Jesus' gaze on you and see the love in his eyes. Jesus' words in verse 21 may seem extreme, but the Gospel-writer Mark is careful to point out they were said in love.

Many people read this passage and feel guilty about identifying with the man who goes away grieving rather than respond to Jesus' call. If this is true for you, bear in mind that Jesus spoke out of love, naming the one thing this particular person needed to grow spiritually. If Jesus were to name the one thing that poses *your* biggest challenge to following him, what might that be?

If you have trouble identifying this one thing, ask God to reveal it to you, but be patient with yourself. Sometimes discernment of this kind of thing takes time.

DAY 4: SIMON THE PHARISEE

Scripture: Luke 7:36-50

Though tradition conflates the woman in this story with Mary Magdalene, this is not Mary Magdalene, who is introduced in the next chapter of Luke. This is someone else. Once again, give this woman the dignity of a name from your own imagination.

First take the part of Simon. How do you feel having Jesus to your house for dinner? How do you feel when the woman enters and begins to wash Jesus' feet? Hear Jesus' words. How do you respond?

Now, take the part of the woman. What has motivated you to minister to Jesus in this way? How do you respond to Jesus' words?

What is the pinch and the promise in this story?

DAY 5: MARTHA AND MARY

Scripture: Luke 10:38-42

Take the roles of Martha and Mary in turn. Many women hearing this story identify with Martha, who wants to make everything nice for her guest and feels frustrated at her family's lack of cooperation. But Mary and Martha are both part of each of us. If you have ever just wanted to sit with Jesus, you too have been Mary, choosing the better part. See if you can imagine not only sitting at Jesus' feet but *wanting nothing more* than to sit at Jesus' feet. What is that like?

Write a prayer in your journal expressing your feelings. Sit quietly for several minutes, imagining being in Jesus' company.

DAY 6: ZACCHAEUS

Scripture: Luke 19:1-10

Imagine you are Zacchaeus. You are rich and have a position of influence but pursue a profession that earns you the contempt of your fellow Jews. Why are you so anxious to see Jesus? What can be so important that you climb a tree to see him? What is the reaction of those around you? Do you care? How does it feel when Jesus calls you by name and invites himself to your house? Do you hear the grumbling of the crowd? What motivates you to pledge your wealth to charity and restitution? Jesus did not ask for this, but he is clearly pleased. How do you feel when he says, "Today salvation has come to this house"?

Imagine Jesus calling you by name and coming to your house. What is it like to host Jesus in your home... and in your heart?

DAY 7: REPETITION

Review the last week, rereading your journal entries. What has stuck with you? What have you learned about Jesus by observing his interactions and conversations? Jesus seems to respond adaptively according to the personalities, needs, and experiences of each person. What happens when you imagine an interaction with Jesus in which he responds to you in your own unique situation?

Thank God for any graces received this week.

WEEK 18

JESUS THE HEALER

During his earthly ministry Jesus was, of course, renowned as a healer as well as a teacher. The healings confirmed his identity as Messiah (Luke 7:18-23) but also grew out of Jesus' great compassion. In the coming week, we will focus on several instances of Jesus healing various physical ailments.

Healing stories may be problematic for those who have prayed for healing for themselves or for loved ones and not experienced cure. On the other hand, you may have experienced or witnessed an unexpected healing yourself. Whatever your experience, this week invites you to consider what healing really is, what kind of healing Jesus offers, and what the implications are for you in following someone whose ministry emphasizes making people whole.

This week, the *grace* is:

To know and experience Jesus' deep compassion and healing presence in order to follow him in his healing ministry.

DAY 1: THE PARALYTIC

Scripture: Mark 2:1-12

Reenact this story in your imagination as the paralytic, then as one of his friends, and finally as one of those who observed the miracle. As the paralytic, what is your sense of what is going on? What do you experience as Jesus pronounces forgiveness? What do you experience when cured of paralysis? How are the experiences of being forgiven and being cured the same and different?

As one of the friends, what is your motivation? What do you expect to happen? Imagine looking down from the roof as Jesus ministers to your friend. What is your reaction to the healing? If you are an observer in the room below, how do you react? How is your perspective different from the friends on the roof?

You may wish to reconstruct the episode taking the part of one of the friends but replacing the paralytic with someone in your own acquaintance today who needs healing. Who are your associates, and how do you decide to bring the person to Jesus together? What lengths would you go to on the possibility that she or he will be healed?

Jesus first forgives the paralytic's sins and physically heals the man only after being challenged by the scribes. What do you make of this?

DAY 2: THE GERASENE DEMONIAC

Scripture: Mark 5:1-20

What do you make of this man's affliction, attributed in the text to "an unclean spirit"? What are your feelings toward him? The man is unsocialized (though we don't know whether that is his choice or the choice of others), violent, erratic, loud, and self-destructive. Have you ever known anyone like that? Even when you have love and pity for such a person, it can be extremely difficult trying to relate and cope. Yet even this person comes to Jesus. Describe how Jesus responds to him. As a disciple or an observer to the action, how do you react?

The people of the city are afraid when they witness the man's rehabilitation. Put yourselves in their place. Why are they afraid?

Jesus often tells people, "Follow me," but though this man begs to follow him, Jesus refuses. Why?

How comfortable are you with following this man's example and proclaiming how much Jesus has done for you?

DAY 3: AN ACCIDENTAL HEALING

Scripture: Mark 5:21-34

Take the part of the woman in this story, suffering for years from something that experts and quacks alike have failed to cure. Feel her discouragement. What moves you to seek out Jesus? Follow the train of thought that leads you to just touch his clothes. Experience the sense of healing. What emotions emerge? Imagine your feelings when Jesus asks, "Who touched me?" In your imagination, come kneel before him and receive his blessing. What is that like?

This healing is unlike the others. It occurs while Jesus' attention is on something else. He is on his way to the bedside of a dying child. He does not consciously encounter this woman. There is no, "What do you want me to do for you?" What does it mean that Jesus heals without even being aware of it? What is this power that emanates from him?

DAY 4: THE SYROPHOENICIAN

Scripture: Mark 7:24-30

According to the text, Jesus was last seen at Gennesaret, on the shores of the Sea of Galilee. What takes him to the region of Tyre, northwest of Galilee on the shores of "the Great Sea" (the Mediterranean) is unknown. Why do you think he might have traveled here, a distance of 20 or 30 miles? Jesus is the foreigner here. As a Syrophoenician, the woman is a native to this area, almost certainly a gentile.

Pretending you are the woman, what brings you to Jesus? Speak to him and hear his response. What feelings arise as he deflects your request?

As harsh as his response may seem, note that he does not say no. What gives you the courage to keep pressing?

What do you experience on returning home and finding your child healed?

DAY 5: THE EPILEPTIC

Scripture: Mark 9:14-29

- "You faithless generation, how much longer must I be with you?"
- "All things can be done for the one who believes."
- "This kind can come out only through prayer."

As in the previous selection, Jesus' words can seem confusing and troubling. How do you react to them? What do you think they mean?

Take the place of the father in this story. What are your hopes and expectations? What do you experience as the disciples fail to heal your child; as Jesus rebukes the spirit; as you see the child convulse and appear to die; and finally as the boy stands up, cured?

Can you identify with the words, "I believe; help my unbelief!"?

DAY 6: THE CENTURION'S SERVANT

Scripture: Luke 7:1-10

It was highly unusual for a Roman soldier to have cordial relations with the Jews in Galilee. Each group typically had nothing but contempt for the other. In this case, however, there is evidence of mutual friendship and even advocacy. Pretend to be the centurion. What appeals to you about the Jewish people in Capernaum, where you are stationed? Slaves were usually considered expendable. Why are you so upset about the illness of this one?

If you are one of the Jewish elders, what is it about the centurion that makes you eager to intercede for him with Jesus?

Jesus praises the centurion's faith. In what ways is your faith like his?

DAY 7: REPETITION

Review the last week, rereading your journal entries. What have you learned about Jesus by participating in his acts of healing? How has your understanding of healing evolved over the past week? What does healing have in common with the forgiveness of sins? For what would you like to be healed? In what ways are you, as a disciple of Jesus, called to be an agent of healing?

Thank God for any graces received this week.

WEEK 19

JESUS THE WORKER OF MIRACLES

Even today there are people who seem to have a "healing touch." But Jesus' power, as reported in the Bible, extends beyond the ability to heal and bends the very laws of nature (what today we would call the laws of physics). What are your thoughts and feelings about miracles?

Faced with Jesus' miracle stories, we in the post-Enlightenment may be tempted to ask, "How did he do that?" Various rational theories have been proposed: Lazarus wasn't really dead; the 5,000 were moved by Jesus' preaching to share food they had brought with them, etc. For the writers of these stories, however, the "how" had been answered. Jesus was the Messiah. He worked his wonders through the power of God.

For us to internalize these stories in order that we may know and follow Jesus, it may be more profitable to ask, "why" than to ask "how." In each of the cases that follow, try to discern what moved Jesus to act in the way that he did. Though few of us have the gift of miracles as Jesus did, we can follow him by being open to the same movements.

This week, the *grace* is:

To observe Jesus' extraordinary powers and discern his motivations, that you may see him more clearly, love him more dearly, and follow him more nearly.

DAY 1: THE MIRACULOUS CATCH OF FISH

Scripture: Luke 5:4-7

We have already worked with the passage to focus on Jesus calling Simon Peter. This time around, concentrate on the miracle of the fishes. Fishing was done at night, and this particular night, Simon and his associates have had no luck at all. Imagine their discouragement and fatigue. Imagine their reaction when this itinerant rabbi tells them to go out again for another try, in the daytime no less, when everybody knows the fish don't bite (or get caught in nets!) And they fill two boats!

Consider why Jesus chose this occasion to demonstrate his miraculous powers and why he chose to act in this way. Have you ever had an occasion of disappointment and failure transformed because of the presence of Jesus? Can you imagine such a thing happening?

DAY 2: CALMING THE STORM

Scripture: Mark 4:35-41

If you have ever felt like the forces of nature were placing you in mortal peril, you have some idea of what the disciples were feeling on this occasion. Yet Jesus is completely unperturbed. What do you make of this?

Are there other kinds of storms that Jesus has the power to still? If there are any "storms" in your life right now, invite Jesus to bring his calming presence to bear.

What does this story say to you about faith and fear?

DAY 3: FEEDING THE CROWDS

Scripture: Mark 6:31-44

Initially, in this story, the hunger that draws people to Jesus is not physical hunger. But after satisfying the people's need for shepherding, Jesus also feeds their bodies. What does this tell you about what it is to follow Jesus?

Record in your journal an experience of small beginnings having unexpectedly large consequences. What does this tell you about God's generosity?

What does the feeding of the 5,000 have in common with the Eucharist for you?

DAY 4: WALKING ON WATER

Scripture: Matthew 14:22-33

What a lot of watery miracles there are!

How would you react, as one of the disciples, seeing Jesus walk on the sea? Why do you suppose Jesus chose to use his power this way? Imagine hearing Jesus' words: "Take heart, it is I; do not be afraid." What effect do these words have on you?

Would you respond as Peter did? Try to imagine what he was feeling as he realized he too was walking on the water, and then panicked and began to sink. Have you ever faltered while trying to reach Jesus? Have you ever felt as if Jesus caught you by the hand as you were sinking? In what tone of voice do you think Jesus says, "You of little faith, why did you doubt?"?

DAY 5: THE WIDOW OF NAIN

Scripture: Luke 7:11-17

This, of course, is not the only time Jesus proves that his power is greater even than the power of death. What does that mean to you?

Several times in the Gospels, Jesus is said to be moved by compassion, as he is in this story. In your journal, write a cinquain about the compassion of Jesus. A cinquain is a five-line poem. Your first line will be the word "compassion." The second line is two adjectives describing Jesus' compassion. The third line will be three adverbs describing Jesus' compassion. The fourth line will be one verb. The fifth will be "Jesus."

DAY 6: "DON'T TELL ANYONE"

Scripture: Mark 1:43-45; Mark 5:43; Mark 7:36; Mark 8:29-30; Luke 5:14

As you can see from the number of citations, miracle stories, particularly in the Gospel of Mark, often conclude with Jesus telling people not to tell anyone. This is known as "the Messianic Secret." Why would Jesus want to keep his miracles quiet? What does this tell you about Jesus?

Have you ever given a gift or done something kind and generous and wished to remain anonymous? If so, what was your motivation? If not, think of anonymous donors and imagine why they want to remain nameless. Could Jesus have been motivated similarly?

DAY 7: REPETITION

Review the last week, rereading your journal entries. What has stuck with you? You have been asked to reflect on why Jesus elected to use his power in each of these miracles. In what kinds of situations does Jesus choose to act miraculously? Are there common threads between these situations? Can you think of any ways in which Jesus' decisions to minister to people can be a model for you in following Jesus?

Thank God for any graces received this week.

WEEK 20

DRAWING CLOSER TO JESUS

In our effort to know Jesus better, we have looked at his teaching, preaching, conversations, and miracles. This week, we narrow the focus to a few events that are especially revealing about who and what Jesus is. As you progress through these readings, try to articulate what Jesus means to you.

This week, the *grace* is:

To observe how Jesus reveals himself to those closest to him, and to listen to what he says about himself, that you may know him better, love him more dearly, and follow him more closely

DAY 1: PETER'S TESTIMONY

Scripture: Mark 8:27-30

As twenty-first century Christians, we have the benefit of knowing the end of Jesus' story. It may be difficult for us to imagine what it was like for the disciples discerning whether Jesus was the Messiah without the evidence of Jesus' death and resurrection. At this point in your journey with Jesus, who do you say that Jesus is? First, imagine what you would say if you were trying to explain to a person who never heard of Jesus who he is to you. Record this in your journal, then imagine you are speaking directly to Jesus as Peter did. In your journal, finish this sentence: "You are…"

DAY 2: THE TRANSFIGURATION

Scripture: Mark 9:2-8

In Jesus' earthly ministry, there is no other event in which Jesus' divinity is more clearly demonstrated than here at the Transfiguration.

Jesus' story could have ended here, with Jesus being swept into heaven without undergoing bodily death, in the manner of the prophet Elijah himself (2 Kings 2:11). How would that have changed Jesus' story and your relationship with him?

What is Peter's motivation in proposing the three dwellings? Can you identify with his sentiments?

DAY 3: THE RAISING OF LAZARUS

Scripture: John 11:1-44

Jesus has already raised other people from death: a little girl (Mark 5:35-43) and the son of the widow of Nain (Luke 7:11-17). How is this narrative the same and different from those other occurrences?

Imagine you are Martha. What are you thinking and feeling as you say, "If you had been here my brother would not have died, but even now I know that God will give you what you ask"? Rehearse the whole conversation. What do you feel within you when you testify to your belief in Jesus being the Messiah, even while Lazarus is still in the tomb? What do you feel when you see Lazarus emerge?

This is one of the rare instances where Jesus' emotional state is described. What does it mean to you that in the context of one of Jesus' most spectacular displays of divine power, Jesus also displays the most human of emotions?

DAY 4: THE BREAD OF LIFE, THE LIGHT OF THE WORLD

Scripture: John 6:35; John 8:12; Exodus 3:14

What does Jesus say about himself? The quotations from John are the first two of seven "I am" statements in that Gospel. They are not only significant because they represent direct self-revelation from Jesus, but because the very "I am" construction recalls the name God gives Godself in Exodus. By using this form, Jesus implicitly identifies himself as divine. But each of the metaphors Jesus uses for himself in the "I am" statements suggests a different facet of his divinity. Ponder each of these metaphors and what they mean to you personally. Feel free to read the larger context of each selection, but then answer from your own experience: How do you experience Jesus as the Bread of Life? How do you experience Jesus as the Light of the World?

DAY 5: THE GATE FOR THE SHEEP, THE GOOD SHEPHERD, THE RESURRECTION AND THE LIFE

Scripture: John 10:7; John 10:11; John 11:25

Jesus is both the sheep-gate and the shepherd. What do these metaphors mean in your relationship with Jesus?

You have, of course, already encountered "I am the Resurrection and the Life" in the story about Lazarus. Having considered other "I am" statements, has your understanding of this statement evolved? If Jesus says, "I am *your* resurrection. I am *your* life," what changes, if anything, in the way you hear this statement?

DAY 6: THE WAY, THE TRUTH, AND THE LIFE; THE VINE

Scripture: John 14:6; John 15:5

What is your understanding of Truth? What does Jesus mean by describing himself as *"The* Truth"? How do you interpret Jesus' words here? If you experience any difficulty with what Jesus is saying, bring your concerns to Jesus in a colloquy and hear how he replies.

Write in your journal about what it means to you to "abide" in Jesus. Reflect on Jesus' stated desire that your joy may be complete (John 15:11). In what ways can you perceive this to be true?

DAY 7: REPETITION

Review the last week, rereading your journal entries. What has stuck with you? Which of the "I am" statements is most meaningful to you?

How has your knowledge of who and what Jesus is evolved over the past several weeks? What have you learned about him? Try to articulate your feelings toward him at this point.

Thank God for any graces received this week.

WEEK 21

WHAT IT MEANS TO FOLLOW JESUS

As Jesus' ministry proceeds, he expects more from his disciples. In this final week before we consider the events of Holy Week and Jesus' Passion, we focus on his teaching on discipleship. Insofar as possible, Jesus wants his followers to know something of what they can expect from following him. Just like the Righteous Leader we met early on in these exercises, Jesus promises his followers both hard work and great reward. He also promises to ask nothing of them that he himself is not also willing to give.

This week the *grace* is:

To hear Jesus' teaching about discipleship, that you may follow him wholeheartedly, intentionally, and faithfully in what lays ahead.

DAY 1: FOXES HAVE HOLES

Scripture: Matthew 8:18-22

How much are you like the scribe in this story, vowing to, and probably truly intending to, follow Jesus wherever he goes? What does Jesus' reply sound like to you?

"Let the dead bury their own dead" sounds harsh but may be another example of rabbinic hyperbole (overstatement to emphasize a point). Bear in mind that the questioner's father is probably not dead awaiting burial but alive and kicking. The person is asking for a postponement of his discipleship until after his father has died. Sometimes there are good reasons to put off something we are called to do, and sometimes we are just making excuses. How can you tell the difference?

DAY 2: CALLING AND SENDING

Scripture: Matthew 10:1, 5-13, 19-20

In the Gospel of Matthew, Jesus no sooner calls his disciples than he sends them out. But before he sends them, he empowers them.

Have you ever had a sense of mission? Describe the experience in your journal. How did it come about, and what did it feel like? Have you ever been empowered or explicitly commissioned to do something? What was that like?

What is your experience of being called by Jesus? Does being called necessarily involve being sent? How has God empowered you? We will return to this subject in the final weeks of these exercises, but what are your thoughts and feelings at this point about being empowered by God?

DAY 3: COSTS

Scripture: Luke 14:27-35

Consider the situation in which the Luke story occurs. Jesus has attracted a massive following. Imagine the range of commitment among such a crowd. Sometimes people follow a movement just because it feels good. And sometimes leaders encourage their followers just because it feels good to be followed. Jesus is not like that. Jesus insists that his followers know something about what they are getting into... that it will not always feel good.

On the other hand, no one can know all the possible consequences of any given decision. If you are married or similarly committed, could you have foreseen at the beginning of that relationship all the challenges that have happened since? What makes it possible to make a commitment given the uncertainty of what the future holds?

What considerations can you see are necessary before committing to following Jesus?

DAY 4: THE PASSION FORETOLD

Scripture: Matthew 16:21-23

This story occurs immediately after Peter has confessed his belief that Jesus is the Messiah (Matthew 16:16). In Peter's place, what would your expectations be about what Jesus is going to do as Messiah? Experience Peter's feelings upon hearing that Jesus plans to head to Jerusalem where he expects to suffer and be killed. What would you say?

Again, Jesus' response is unexpectedly harsh. Jesus has just blessed Peter and named him the "rock" upon which the church will be founded (Matthew 16:18-19). Now he calls him "Satan" and "stumbling block." As Peter, how do you interpret this?

DAY 5: THE PASSION FORETOLD AGAIN

Scripture: Luke 9:43b-45; Luke 18:31-34

Twice more, Jesus tells the disciples of what lays ahead. Why has he had to repeat himself? What is different for you, if anything, in each telling?

Have you ever had difficulty grasping an uncomfortable truth or some unwelcome news? What made it so hard? How is it possible to accept something you must know but don't want to hear?

DAY 6: CROSS, BAPTISM AND CUP

Scripture: Matthew 16:24-26; Mark 10:35-45

What is it to take up one's cross? Notice that Jesus does not say, "the cross" or "my cross," but says that followers must take up "their cross." What does that mean to you? What is *your* cross? How can losing your life for Jesus' sake also be finding your life?

What do the following words mean to you as they are used in the Mark passage:

- glory

- cup

- baptism

- slave

- ransom

Write your reflections in your journal, even if just as a stream of consciousness.

DAY 7: REPETITION

Review the last week, rereading your journal entries. What has stuck with you? How does Jesus' teaching on the costs of discipleship and his predicting of his Passion influence your picture of him?

As Jesus approaches Jerusalem for the last time, what do you suppose his frame of mind is? How are the disciples feeling? How are you feeling about Jesus? Have a colloquy with Jesus in which you share your feelings at this stage of his story and listen for his reply. Close your prayer session with the "Our Father," and sense Jesus praying with you.

Thank God for any graces received this week.

PART IV

GREAT LOVE, GREAT SUFFERING

STABAT MATER

Latin, 13th Century

At the cross her vigil keeping,
stood the mournful mother weeping,
where he hung, the dying Lord:
there she waited in her anguish,
seeing Christ in torment languish,
in her heart the piercing sword.

With what pain and desolation,
with what grief and resignation,
Mary watched her dying son.
Deep the woe of her affliction,
when she saw the crucifixion
of the sole begotten one.

Him she saw for our salvation
mocked with cruel acclamation,
scourged, and crowned with thorns entwined;
saw him then from judgment taken,
and in death by all forsaken,
till his spirit he resigned.

Who, on Christ's dear mother gazing,

pierced by anguish so amazing,

born of woman, would not weep?

Who, on Christ's dear mother thinking,

such a cup of sorrow drinking,

would not share her sorrows deep?

Jesus, may her deep devotion

stir in me the same emotion,

Fount of love, Redeemer kind;

that my heart fresh ardor gaining,

And a purer love attaining,

may with thee acceptance find.

©The Church Pension Fund, 1985, Church Publishing Incorporated.

Our journey with Jesus has brought us to the brink of the Passion. This can be a difficult time. I know people who avoid going to church on Palm Sunday because that is when the Passion narrative is read. It is hard to hear about anyone, especially Jesus, treated so brutally and so unjustly. It is harder still to be made to take part in the angry crowd that shouts, "Crucify him!"

Why put ourselves through this? The simple answer is that there is no miracle of resurrection without death. Another reason is that the Passion shows us dim humans once and for all what kind of God we have.

The following parable is widely distributed on the internet

anonymously. It expresses much wisdom, and to me suggests one answer to why Jesus had to suffer so much.

An addict fell in a hole and couldn't get out. A businessman went by, and the addict called out for help. The businessman threw him some money and told him to buy himself a ladder. But the addict could not buy a ladder in the hole he was in.

A doctor walked by. The addict said, "Help! I can't get out!" The doctor gave him some drugs and said, "Take this. It will relieve the pain." The addict said thanks, but when the pills ran out, he was still in the hole.

A well-known psychiatrist rode by and heard the addict's cries for help. He stopped and asked, "How did you get here? Were you born there? Did your parents put you there? Tell me about yourself, it will alleviate your sense of loneliness." So the addict talked with him for an hour, then the psychiatrist had to leave, but he said he'd come back next week. The addict thanked him, but he was still in the hole.

A priest came by. The addict called for help. The priest gave him a Bible and said, "I'll say a prayer for you." He got down on his knees and prayed for the addict, then he left. The addict was very grateful; he read the Bible, but he was still stuck in the hole.

A recovering addict happened to be passing by. The addict cried out, "Hey, help me. I'm stuck in this hole!" Right away, the recovering addict jumped down in the hole with him. The addict said, "What are you doing? Now we're both stuck here!" But the recovering addict said, "Calm down. It's okay. I've been here before. I know how to get out."

In a very real way, Jesus is the recovering addict in this story, jumping into the hole of human suffering to show the rest of us the way out. A Messiah who doesn't suffer might be adequate if we humans did not suffer. But we do. And to redeem and sanctify every iota of human experience, Jesus enters our suffering, suffering so extremely that nothing we may experience will be something unknown by God. "We do not have a high priest who is unable to sympathize with our weaknesses." (Hebrews 4:15). In a very real way, Jesus suffers for our sake. Jesus suffers for your sake.

By suffering, Jesus is able to accompany us in our suffering. Praying the Passion is one way to reciprocate, accompanying Jesus in *his* suffering. But further, an interesting thing happens when we identify with Jesus' suffering. Just as Jesus' suffering is redemptive, by identifying with Jesus we come to see our own suffering as potentially redemptive. This is part of the healing and transformation we seek in these exercises.

Jesus approached Jerusalem for the final time in humility. In imitation of Jesus, and following Ignatius' pattern, we preface our journey with Jesus to Jerusalem with a contemplation on what Ignatius calls "The Three Kinds of Humility."

PRAYER EXERCISES

- Dispose yourself for prayer.

- Breathe deeply, at least one cleansing breath.

- Pray for the grace of the week.

- Read through the entire day's prompt before

beginning the first step.

- Practice lectio divina with the Scripture passages.

- Journal your answers to each day's prayer prompts, or otherwise as you are moved.

- Offer your reflections to God in prayer.

- Do not forget to do your daily examen sometime before bed.

WEEK 22

PREPARATIONS

This week, the *grace* is:

To prepare for Jesus' entry into our hearts and his giving of himself at the Passover meal.

DAY 1: HUMILITY

Reading:

> *Humility lies in the acceptance of Jesus Christ as the fullness of what it means to be human. To be humble is to live as close to the truth as possible: that I am created to the likeness of Christ, that I am meant to live according to the pattern of his paschal mystery, and that my whole fulfillment is found in being as near to Christ as he draws me to himself.*[32]

We introduced some of Ignatius' concepts of humility in the section on the First Principle and Foundation and revisited them in Week 5, Day 2. Ignatius returns to the subject of humility before presenting his "Third Week," which deals with the Passion of Christ. Here he describes "Three Kinds of Humility." The first kind of humility is obedience to the law of God in all things. The second is indifference to wealth or poverty, honor or dishonor, long or short life, in deference to the service of God and one's own salvation. The third is imitation of Christ to the point of poverty and humiliation if such a choice serves and praises the glory of God.

Ignatius' standards may seem lofty and unattainable. Remember that humility is a journey, and that it has its roots in the desire to please God. Consider this prayer of Thomas Merton's:

---

[32] Fleming, *Exercises*, 101.

My Lord God, I have no idea where I am going. I do not see the road ahead of me. I cannot know for certain where it will end. Nor do I really know myself, and the fact that I think that I am following your will does not mean that I am actually doing so. But I believe that the desire to please you does in fact please you. And I hope I have that desire in all that I am doing. I hope that I will never do anything apart from that desire. And I know that if I do this you will lead me by the right road, though I may know nothing about it. Therefore will I trust you always, though I may seem to be lost and in the shadow of death. I will not fear, for you are ever with me, and you will never leave me to face my perils alone.[33]

Pray this prayer if it has resonance with you. Then, in your journal, define what humility means to you, and describe where you are in your experience of personal humility.

DAY 2: THE ENTRY INTO JERUSALEM

Scripture: Matthew 21:1-11; Zechariah 9:9-10

Jesus has approached Jerusalem expecting persecution. But this day at least he enters in triumph. Imagine the Place. What do you feel as a member of the crowd? What do you understand about this person on the donkey? As a disciple, what are you feeling? What do you expect will happen in the week ahead on the basis of this reception?

---

[33] "The Merton Prayer" from *Thoughts in Solitude* Copyright © 1956, 1958 by the Abbey of Our Lady of Gethsemani, (downloaded from https://reflections.yale.edu/article/seize-day-vocation-calling-work/merton-prayer, October 20, 2021.)

Consider the reference from the prophet Zechariah, where the donkey is contrasted with the war-horse. What kind of King is Jesus? What kind of triumph and victory is this?

DAY 3: CLEANSING THE TEMPLE (MATTHEW)

Scripture: Matthew 21:10-13

In the Gospel of Matthew, Jesus goes directly from his triumphal entry to the cleansing of the Temple. We considered John's account of the cleansing of the Temple in Week 13, Day 6. John places this story at the beginning of Jesus' ministry. Matthew (along with Mark and Luke) places it near the end. At this point in the story, Jesus has entered Jerusalem knowing his life is in danger. On the other hand, he is fresh off an exuberant public welcome. How do these factors influence your reaction as you observe the action in the Temple unfold?

DAY 4: PREDICTING THE TEMPLE'S DESTRUCTION

Scripture: Mark 13:1-2

For most Jews, a journey to Jerusalem was a solemn, eagerly anticipated, and joyous occasion. In addition, the Temple, by all accounts, was a truly impressive building. As a disciple, what do you make of Jesus' speech here? These are words that will be used against Jesus when he comes to trial. Try to imagine being one of the people who takes offense at Jesus' words. What if Jesus were to say these words about your beloved place of worship? Is there anything in what Jesus says or does in any point of his ministry that arouses in you the same resistance felt by his listeners on this occasion?

DAY 5: CONSPIRACY AND BETRAYAL

Scripture: Matthew 26:1-5, 14-16

No one can say that Jesus neglects to inform his disciples what lies ahead. Why do they have such trouble understanding? Have you ever been in a situation where you resisted the inevitability of something you were told was going to happen?

What emotions arise in you reading about the treachery of the chief priests and elders, and the betrayal of Judas? What do you think would happen if you warned Jesus of these developments?

DAY 6: PREPARING FOR PASSOVER

Scripture: Mark 14:12-16

Think of the annual liturgical events that require preparation on your part. Make a mental list of the things you typically do for such an event. What is your frame of mind as you make these preparations? If you can do this, you will have an idea of what the disciples are feeling at this point in the story.

What do you make of the directions about following the man with the jar? Has Jesus made prior arrangements or is he exercising prophetic powers? Does it make a difference?

DAY 7: REPETITION

Review the last week, rereading your journal entries. Our theme this week was to prepare for Jesus' entry into our hearts and for his self-giving at the Last Supper. What part has humility had in your preparation? How has following Jesus through his last week in Jerusalem affected you? For what, if anything, has it prepared you? What is your state of heart and mind as we go forward?

WEEK 23

THE LAST SUPPER

This week the *grace* is:

To experience intimacy with Christ as he serves, feeds, teaches, and shares himself with you.

DAY 1: WASHING

Scripture: John 13:1-14

John is the only Gospel to relate the story of Jesus washing the disciples' feet. Consider everything that may be going on within Jesus' consciousness here: he knows his death is immanent, he is determined to love his own till the end, he is aware of Judas' betrayal, and he knows "that the Father had given all things into his hands and that he had come from God and was going to God." Feel the weight of all that knowledge. Reflect that it is within the context of all those considerations that Jesus gets up to do the work of a servant. What feelings does this arouse in you?

Rehearse the conversation between Peter and Jesus. Would you have reacted the way Peter did?

How does Jesus' action here influence the understanding of humility you wrote about last week?

DAY 2: "IS IT I?"

Scripture: Mark 14:17-21

Mark reports that when Jesus reveals that one of the disciples will betray him, their reaction is one of sorrow. Is that the reaction you would expect? What is the cause of the disciples' sorrow here? Why do they each respond by asking, "Is it I?" Imagine asking Jesus, "Is it I?" What is in your heart as you ask this? If Jesus were to answer, what would he say?

DAY 3: BODY AND BLOOD

Scripture: Mark 14:22-25

These words are so familiar in the words of the Eucharist that their impact on the original disciples may be hard to conceptualize. Nevertheless, try to imagine hearing these words for the first time. What goes through your mind?

Ignatius observes that during the Passion, Jesus the God-man hides his divinity (SE196).[34] In the giving of his body and blood in the Eucharist, is Jesus revealing his humanity or his divinity?

If you were asked what the Eucharist means to you, what would you say?

DAY 4: GLORY

Scripture: John 13:31-32

We tend to think of Jesus coming into his glory after his resurrection. Here Jesus says, "Now the Son of Man has been glorified," immediately after Judas leaves the place to betray Jesus to his enemies. What does this suggest to you? In what does Jesus' glory exist? In what sense does any aspect of Jesus' suffering contribute to his glory?

Can any aspect of the suffering you have known in your own life ever be considered glory?

---

[34] Ignatius, *Exercises*, 64.

DAY 5: A NEW COMMANDMENT

Scripture: John 13:33-35

Jesus has been preaching love throughout his ministry. What is "new" about this commandment? What is the significance of Jesus speaking of this in the context of the Last Supper?

There's an old aphorism that goes, "If you were arrested for being a Christian, would there be enough evidence to convict you?" What feelings arise in you when you hear that everyone will know whether we are disciples if we have love for one another? What might people think of us by the way we treat each other?

DAY 6: FRIENDS

Scripture: John 15:12-17

"Oh, what a friend we have in Jesus," goes the old hymn. We are taught to think of Jesus as our friend. What does it add to hear Jesus explicitly call *you* his friend? Have a colloquy with Jesus in which you ask him what he means when he calls you "friend."

What do you hear when Jesus says, "I chose you"?

DAY 7: REPETITION

Review the last week, rereading your journal entries. How has your concept of the Last Supper evolved as a result of your study this week? Spend a final few moments cherishing the intimacy of this last meal with Jesus. What do you want to take with you as we move forward?

WEEK 24

IN THE GARDEN

This week, the *grace* is:

To enter into the sorrow and suffering of Christ in order to understand the vast extent of his love and mercy.

DAY 1: PETER'S DENIAL FORETOLD

Scripture: Matthew 26:30-35

As we move forward, it will be important to keep the focus on Jesus. In the case of today's exercise, this means focusing less on Peter and the disciples (and the rest of us who let Jesus down) and more on what it is like for Jesus to remain faithful and compassionate while being betrayed by those he loves. How do you think Jesus feels toward Peter at this moment? If you were there to comfort Jesus, what would you say?

DAY 2: PRAYER IN GETHSEMANE

Scripture: Matthew 26:36-46; Luke 22:39-46

Matthew and Luke highlight different elements of the story of the agony in the garden. Matthew includes three occasions of Jesus returning to find the disciples sleeping. Verses in Luke describe the ministration of an angel and tell of Jesus sweating blood in his distress. What does each version add, for you? Luke also attributes the disciples' sleepiness to grief. What are the disciples grieving at this point?

If you had been a disciple, how would you feel about Jesus leaving you to pray alone? Would you have wanted to go with him? What would you have said to him?

At the beginning of Part IV, we spoke of humility. What does Jesus' prayer, "Remove this cup from me, but not my will but yours be done," say about his brand of humility?

DAY 3: ARREST

Scripture: Matthew 26:47-50; John 18:2-9

Once again, we have two slightly different views of the story. What does each suggest to you?

As one of the disciples present, how do you feel when Judas comes forward to kiss Jesus? What does Judas' kiss represent to you?

DAY 4: THE SWORD

Scripture: Matthew 26:51-54; Luke 22:49-51

Some of the disciples respond to Jesus' arrest with violence. What is your feeling about this? Would you have been similarly inclined? In Matthew, Jesus uses this as a teaching moment. In Luke, it is one last opportunity for Jesus to perform a healing. If you were there, how would you take Jesus' claim that the Father could deliver him at that moment? Would Jesus' argument about accepting his arrest to fulfill the scriptures move you?

DAY 5: THE POWER OF DARKNESS

Scripture: Luke 22:52-53

What does "the power of darkness" mean to you in the context of Jesus' arrest? What does it mean to you in your own experience? What is the relationship between Jesus' darkness and your darkness?

DAY 6: FORSAKEN

Scripture: Mark 14:50-52

Write a cinquain about Jesus' experience in the Garden of Gethsemane:

- First line: "Jesus"
- Second line: two adjectives describing Jesus in the Garden
- Third line: three adverbs (word ending "-ly") applicable to the scene
- Fourth line: one verb
- Fifth line: "Forsaken"

DAY 7: REPETITION

We have spent the whole week on the last few hours of Jesus' life before his arrest. Review your entries of the last week. What have you learned about Jesus by observing him in adversity? What are your thoughts and feelings about Jesus' humility? What is the grace to be found in this sad context?

WEEK 25

TRIAL AND CRUCIFIXION

We are about to spend an entire week following Jesus through events that took place over a matter of hours in real time. This may seem excessive, especially given that the material is so difficult. The point is to observe how Jesus remains true to himself and his mission throughout his trials, and to consider what great love enables him to do this. Remember that this love is personal. This love is for you.

This week, the prayer prompts are shorter than usual. At this point it is not necessary to write a lot in your journal. The important thing in your prayer this week is simply to be with Jesus. Accompany him in his pain that you may know truly how closely he accompanies you in yours.

This week the grace is:

To enter into the sorrow and suffering of Christ in order to understand the vast extent of his love and mercy.

DAY 1: FALSE TESTIMONY AND ABUSE

Scripture: Mark 14:55-65

Observe Jesus' accusers and tormenters. What are they motivated by? Now look at Jesus and observe how he refuses to return insult for insult. Even under extreme duress, he remains true to himself and to his mission. Consider again how Jesus hides his divinity and reveals his divinity at the same time.

It is hard to observe someone being mistreated, but if this exercise excites compassion within you for Jesus, consider that you are feeling something that was central to Jesus' being. You are sharing in Jesus' love.

DAY 2: PETER'S DENIAL

Scripture: Luke 22:54-62

Peter at least does not abandon Jesus immediately. What is he thinking and feeling as he follows the crowd to the high priest's house? He hangs around for a long time, even though it is increasingly clear people are recognizing him as Jesus' associate. Why? Think of that glance between Jesus and Peter. Imagine Jesus' face at that moment. What does Peter see there?

Day 3: Before Pilate

Scripture: Luke 23:1-5

Observe Jesus before Pilate. Once again, imagine Jesus' face. What is the source of Pilate's power? What is the source of Jesus'? Who seems stronger here?

DAY 4: BEFORE HEROD

Scripture: Luke 23:6-12

Herod has heard about Jesus and has expectations of him that Jesus refuses to fulfill. Jesus' failure to play Herod's game seems to excite anger and cruelty. Why does Jesus "give no answer"? Again, concentrate on Jesus' face. What do you see there?

DAY 5: "WHAT IS TRUTH?"

Scripture: John 18:33-38a

John is the Gospel-writer most likely to record entire conversations. Rehearse this conversation between Jesus and Pilate. What is Pilate's attitude toward Jesus? What is Jesus' attitude toward Pilate? Where is the truth in this exchange?

DAY 6: SENTENCE

Scripture: John 18:38b-19:16

Observe the movement within Pilate as his conversation with Jesus continues. What does Pilate see in Jesus, and what does he hear in his words? What do *you* see and hear from Jesus in this exchange?

DAY 7: REPETITION

Review the last week, rereading your journal entries. What conclusions do you draw about Jesus after following him so closely through his trials? How does Jesus' suffering relate to your own suffering? For Jesus, suffering is a source of compassion for others. How can your suffering become a source of compassion for others? How can your compassion for Jesus translate into compassion for all?

Thank God for any graces received this week.

WEEK 26

DEATH AND BURIAL

This week the *grace* is:

To enter into the sorrow and suffering of Christ in order to understand the vast extent of his love and mercy.

DAY 1: CRUCIFIXION

Scripture: Mark 15:21-23; Luke 23:33-35; John 19:16-25a

At times of deep emotion, words alone cannot express what we are feeling. Music often helps. Borrow a hymnal from your church if you don't have one at home, or search online and find a Good Friday hymn that expresses your feelings about seeing Jesus on the cross. Copy it into your journal and pray it.

DAY 2: TAUNTS

Scripture: Matthew 27:39-43; Luke 23:36-37

What is it that inspires human beings to kick people when they are down? What emotions arise in you when you observe the people in the story literally adding insult to injury? Express your sorrow about human cruelty to Jesus in prayer.

DAY 3: "REMEMBER ME"

Scripture: Luke 23:39-43

What does it tell you about Jesus that even in abject pain, he offers comfort to another anguished soul?

DAY 4: "HERE IS YOUR MOTHER"

Scripture: John 19:25b-27

What is Jesus doing for these two broken-hearted people? What does that say about Jesus' calling to those of us who would follow him?

DAY 5: DEATH

Scripture: Mark 15:33-39; Luke 23:44-47

At Jesus' birth, according to the Christmas carol, "heaven and nature sing." Here at his death heaven and nature tear their clothes, the traditional demonstration of grief. What does this tell you about the relationship between Jesus and creation?

DAY 6: BURIAL

Scripture: Mark 15:42-47

Crucified prisoners could be left on the cross to rot as a warning to others not to challenge the Roman Empire. For Pilate to allow Joseph of Arimathea to entomb Jesus, however hurriedly to avoid profaning the Sabbath, was a significant mercy. What difference do small acts of charity make in the context of great tragedy?

DAY 7: REPETITION

Review your journal entries for the past week, and for this whole section on Jesus' Passion. What have you learned about the vastness of Christ's love and mercy from entering into Jesus' sorrow?

PART V

RISING AND ASCENDING

I THANK YOU GOD FOR MOST THIS AMAZING

e. e. cummings

i thank You God for most this amazing

day: for the leaping greenly spirits of trees

and a blue true dream of sky; and for everything

which is natural which is infinite which is yes

(i who have died am alive again today,

and this is the sun's birthday; this is the birth

day of life and love and wings: and of the gay

great happening illimitably earth)

how should tasting touching hearing seeing

breathing any- lifted from the no

of all nothing- human merely being

doubt unimaginable You?

(now the ears of my ears awake and

now the eyes of my eyes are opened)

Alleluia! Christ is risen! The Lord is risen indeed!

Finally!

Many churches celebrate Easter with a sunrise service. How appropriate this is! A new day is dawning.

As I write this, my family has just returned from a reunion on the Outer Banks of North Carolina. Even though we were on vacation, nearly all of us got up extra early every day to watch the sun rise over the ocean. It was different and dazzling and wondrous each time. Looking down the beach, we could see other families doing the same thing. I reflected that in an age when electronic amusements are available literally at the touch of a button, people continue to seek a spectacle that has repeated itself daily over millions of years. And after millions of years, it is still new every day.

You undoubtedly have experienced Easter many times. But each Easter is a new beginning. As we observe Easter in these exercises, whether or not the timing coincides with Easter in "real time" for you, prepare for newness in your soul. If you are able, begin this section with another prophetic action: Get up early to watch the sun rise. Observe how the first rays fill you with anticipation. As the sun breaks the horizon, note how everything you see is transformed.

This is the power of resurrection. This is how Jesus transforms everything. Including you.

PRAYER EXERCISES

- Dispose yourself for prayer.
- Breathe deeply, at least one cleansing breath.
- Pray for the grace of the week.
- Read through the entire day's prompt before beginning the first step.
- Practice *lectio divina* with the Scripture passages.

- Journal your answers to each day's prayer prompts, or otherwise as you are moved.

- Offer your reflections to God in prayer.

- Do not forget to do your daily examen sometime before bed.

WEEK 27

RESURRECTION

For those of us familiar with the story, Jesus' resurrection comes as a huge relief after all the horror and grief of his passion and death. The first witnesses, however, experienced a different range of emotions: terror, disbelief, amazement, false assumptions, misunderstanding, clinging, doubt. By immersing ourselves in their stories, we may enhance our understanding of how stupendous the resurrection really is. Read their accounts in the days and weeks ahead. Witness the process by which people come to understand and rejoice in Jesus' triumph. Each person experiences conversion anew, and nothing for them is ever the same again. As you rejoice in the resurrection, pray that the wonder and glory of this stupendous event may bring about such a conversion in you.

This week, the *grace* is:

> To experience awe and wonder at the stupendous resurrection of Jesus.

DAY 1: NEWNESS

Scripture: 2 Corinthians 5:17

There can be no greater contrast between last week and the glory of Easter. Is this an easy transition for you, or do you need time to adjust? In the days to come, we will see that many of the first witnesses to the resurrection needed time to adjust. Apparently it has always been true that people come to Jesus in different ways. How do you come to the resurrected Jesus? Do you rush into his arms or approach carefully? Have a colloquy with Jesus in which you imagine conversing with him for the first time after his resurrection. What do you say, and how does he reply?

DAY 2: DESCENT TO THE DEAD

Reading:

> *His soul, likewise united with the divinity, descended into hell.*
> *There he sets free the souls of the just...* (SE 219)[35]

Scripture: Ezekiel 37:1-14

Christian tradition holds that before his resurrection appearances on earth, Jesus descended to hell to free the righteous dead. This act is known as the "Harrowing of Hell" and is referenced in the Apostles' Creed.

At the very least, this doctrine demonstrates that Jesus' resurrection is even more than the miracle of a dead individual returning to life. The significance of the resurrection is cosmic, extending beyond history and even beyond what we now refer to as the laws of physics. In Jesus, everything, including death itself (proverbially the one thing that never changes), is transformed.

Practice lectio divina with the passage from Ezekiel. What does it mean to you that God "brings people up from their graves"?

DAY 3: JESUS THE CONSOLER

Reading:

> *He appeared to the Virgin Mary. Though this is not mentioned*
> *explicitly in the Scripture it must be considered as stated when*
> *Scripture says that He appeared to many others.* (SE 299).[36]

---

[35] Ignatius, *Exercises*, 73.

[36] Ignatius, *Exercises*, 107.

Ignatius assumed that the resurrected Jesus, in his great compassion, would first visit his mother, the person who probably suffered most by seeing Jesus tortured and killed. As Ignatius himself notes, there is no explicit scriptural reference for this. But if it happened as Ignatius imagined, what would this add to your understanding of Jesus? If you are able, imagine the reunion between mother and son. Alternatively, imagine a joyful reunion you yourself have experienced. How do your feelings on that occasion compare to your joy at the resurrection of Jesus?

DAY 4: TERROR

Scripture: Mark 16:1-8

In Mark's account, the women flee from the tomb in terror, saying "nothing to anyone." The oldest and most reliable sources for the Gospel of Mark end here. Verses 9-20 are believed to be a later addition to Mark's account by another hand, and scholars doubt its authenticity.

Put yourself in the place of one of the women. Imagine the place. Imagine your feelings and expectations as you approach the tomb, conversing with your friends. What do you feel as you notice that the stone has been moved? As you enter the tomb? As you see the "young man dressed in white" and hear his words? Do you feel "terror and amazement" or something else? Record your experience in your journal.

DAY 5: CONVEYING THE MESSAGE

Scripture: Luke 24:1-9

In Luke's account, there are "two men in dazzling clothes," and their message contains a reminder of Jesus' teaching. Like Mark, Luke reports that the women are terrified, but here they manage to convey to the disciples the message with which they are entrusted. Have you ever had a task to fulfill even though you were very scared? Recall such an event in order to put yourself, once again, in the place of one of these women. If you were there, what would you believe?

DAY 6: DISBELIEF

Scripture: Scripture: Luke 24:10-12

This isn't the first time that women are disbelieved, and it won't be the last. If you are one of the women, how do you feel that your report is considered "an idle tale"?

The disciples don't believe, but according to verse 12 (which does not appear in all Bibles), Peter at least gets up to check out the empty tomb. Now, imagine you are Peter. What are you thinking and feeling as you set out for the tomb and find it empty except for the discarded burial linens?

DAY 7: REPETITION

Review your journal entries for the past week. What has impressed or stuck with you? Revisit any moments of particular grace.

Excepting the non-scriptural account of Jesus appearing to his mother, no one alive in our accounts so far has yet seen the resurrected

Jesus. In a way, Christians today are in the same boat as Jesus' friends early on that first Easter morning. None of us has seen the resurrected Jesus in the flesh. This being the case, what is it that enables *you* to believe that Jesus could rise from the dead?

WEEK 28

MARY MAGDALENE

This week, the *grace* is:

With Mary Magdalene, to experience great joy at hearing that Jesus has risen, and to hear Jesus call you by name.

DAY 1: FEAR AND GREAT JOY

Scripture: Matthew 28:1-8

We are going to spend the next week with Mary Magdalene, the most faithful of Jesus' disciples, on the morning of Jesus' resurrection. All of the Gospels credit her with being one of the first to see Jesus, though they differ in their accounts. We will not try to harmonize these accounts but will consider them in turn to derive fruit from each version. Remember that when the Bible is confusing, good questions to ask are, "What truth is there here for me? What might God want to communicate to me here?" What is the truth for you in each of the versions of Mary's experience on the first Easter morning?

In Matthew, Mary leaves the empty tomb in "fear and great joy." Try to imagine what her fear and great joy feel like. Have you ever felt anything like the simultaneous combination of these two emotions? Make a list in your journal of adjectives that might describe such an experience.

DAY 2: ASSUMPTIONS

Scripture: John 20:1-2

In John's account, Mary does not encounter an angel in the empty tomb. She observes that the seal has been disturbed and jumps to the conclusion that Jesus' body has been stolen: "They have taken the Lord." Putting yourself in her place, why would you think this?

DAY 3: MISUNDERSTANDING

Scripture: John 20:3-10

According to John, Peter and the other disciple do not discredit Mary's report as they do in Luke, but they're not exactly converted either. John tells us the other disciple sees and believes but doesn't understand that Jesus must rise from the dead. It appears all he believes at this point is that the tomb is empty. What are he and Peter thinking and feeling?

What do you think of the fact that even the people closest to Jesus were confused? What light, if any, does their experience of confusion and misunderstanding shed on your own moments of confusion and misunderstanding?

DAY 4: NOT RECOGNIZING

Scripture: John 20:11-15

Put yourself in Mary's place. Why didn't she recognize Jesus at first? Have there been times in your life where you only recognized the voice/face/presence of God in retrospect? Describe the experience in your journal.

DAY 5: CALLED BY NAME

Scripture: John 20:16

What is the significance of Jesus calling Mary by name? Imagine Jesus calling you by name. What is your reaction at hearing your name from his mouth?

Where and how do you recognize the presence of God in your life today? If you have ever had a breakthrough in your faith, what was it that contributed to that experience? Can you think of that breakthrough as Jesus calling you by name?

DAY 6: HOLDING

Scripture: John 20:17-18

Mary is obviously moved to embrace Jesus. Imagine the moment. What tone of voice does Jesus use in saying, "Do not hold on to me"? Allow yourself to feel what Mary must be feeling in this scene. What do you take his words to mean?

Are there good ways to hold on and bad ways to hold on? What are the ways you hold on to Jesus?

DAY 7: REPETITION

Review the last week, rereading your journal entries. How has your concept of the first Easter evolved as you have walked in the sandals of Mary Magdalene? Have a colloquy with Mary Magdalene in which you ask her about her first encounter with the resurrected Jesus.

Revisit any moments of particular grace. Say a prayer of thanksgiving to Mary for guiding you this week.

WEEK 29

A WIDENING CIRCLE

This week, the *grace* is:

For your joy to grow and expand as the circle of those encountering the resurrected Jesus grows and expands.

DAY 1: PEACE BE WITH YOU

Scripture: John 20:19-23

Imagine the atmosphere in that fear-filled room. Take the place of one of the disciples, suddenly seeing Jesus in your midst. Hear his invitation to inspect his hands and side. What do you do? Do you draw near for a closer look? Feel the joy rising within yourself and amongst your comrades. Feel Jesus' breath and hear his words. What do you make of what Jesus says about the Holy Spirit and about forgiveness?

DAY 2: THOMAS

Scripture: John 20:24-25

As we have seen in other passages, people who hear about Jesus' rising without visual proof have trouble believing the news. Pretend you are Thomas, returning home and finding your associates jumping for joy at something you have missed. Describe your feelings. Would you have reacted as skeptically as Thomas did?

DAY 3: CONVERSION

Scripture: John 20:26-29

Can you imagine what that week must have been like for Thomas? As Thomas, what do you feel when Jesus finally appears? What do you feel when he invites you to touch his wounds? The scripture implies that Thomas, in the end, did not need the tactile proof he had said would be necessary for him to believe. Repeat Thomas' words aloud, "My Lord and my God!" What emotions arise in you as you say them?

Jesus goes on to say, "Blessed are those who have not seen and yet have come to believe." How do you relate to these words?

DAY 4: BREAKING BREAD

Scripture: Luke 24:13-32

Imagine the place: the Emmaus Road. Take the part of one of the two friends lamenting Jesus' death as you walk along. You are joined by a stranger. Let the scene play out as described. What are you feeling as Jesus speaks about a Messiah who must suffer? You come to the inn and persuade your strange companion to join you. Imagine sitting down to dinner together. Observe the handling, blessing, breaking, and giving of bread. What is there about this action that causes you to finally recognize Jesus?

Describe in your journal any experience you may have had in your own life of Jesus being made known in the breaking of the bread.

DAY 5: JOY MIXED WITH DISBELIEF

Scripture: Luke 24:33-43

This is Luke's version of Jesus' first appearance to the assembled disciples. Imagine you are there, hearing the story from the two travelers who met Jesus on the road to Emmaus. You speak of Jesus appearing to Simon (an event Luke has somehow failed to describe). Why are you so startled and terrified when Jesus appears? Why might it be easier to believe in ghosts than that Jesus might have risen?

After Jesus displays his wounds, the disciples are described as joyful, but still disbelieving and wondering. How is it possible to feel all these emotions at one time?

DAY 6: OPENING THE MIND

Scripture: Luke 24:44-48

As he did with the Emmaus travelers, Jesus now goes through the scriptures, pointing out references to a Messiah who must suffer. Luke says Jesus "opened their minds." Imagine the sensation. Have you ever experienced a comparable enlightenment? In your journal, describe what that was like.

Which do you think is more important: an open mind or an open heart?

Pray for openness to the risen Jesus.

DAY 7: REPETITION

Review the last week, rereading your journal entries. Revisit moments of particular grace.

You have taken the roles of those closest to Jesus as they react to actually seeing him resurrected. Now just be yourself. In your own words, describe your personal feelings at knowing that Jesus has risen from the dead. You may just want to make a list of adjectives. Or choose your favorite Easter hymn and copy it into your journal, underlining the words that have special meaning to you.

WEEK 30

MISSION APPEARANCES

Jesus, appearing to his friends after his resurrection, does several things: first he comforts and reassures, since people are understandably startled and even afraid. Then, often, he reviews the scriptures that foretold a savior who would suffer. Finally, he sends his listeners out to spread the news of his rising and the message of his gospel. In this section we concentrate on the stories where Jesus conveys a sense of mission to his disciples. As you read these passages, imagine Jesus speaking these words to you.

This week, the *grace* is:

To feel great joy at knowing that Jesus lives and to listen to his call to mission.

DAY 1: FISHING

Scripture: John 21:1-8

Scholars believe that this account may be written by a different hand than the preceding chapters, and that it originally existed independently from them. This may explain why the disciples in this story are back in Galilee fishing as if they never saw the risen Jesus in the locked room as described in Chapter 20. Do not worry about harmonizing these two accounts. Take this one about fishing on the Sea of Tiberias (Galilee) on its own merits. As always, the point is not to try to make the Bible make sense according to your own lights, but to listen for the truth in each passage.

Imagine you are a disciple trying to make sense of your life after Jesus' death. In this context, why might the option of returning to a familiar activity appeal to you?

This account has many parallels to Luke 5:1-11: the night of fruitless fishing followed by a miraculous catch. Here the event is more about recognition than about discovery: The disciples recognize a Jesus they already know rather than encountering him for the first time as they do in Luke.

Are you more like Peter, impetuously jumping into the water, or more like the disciples who stay in the boat to drag the teeming net to shore?

What is it like to recognize Jesus after a period of separation? Has anything similar ever happened to you?

DAY 2: COME AND HAVE BREAKFAST

Scripture: John 21:9-14

A miracle has occurred (two miracles, if you include the resurrection itself), and Jesus makes the homely suggestion of just having breakfast. What are your thoughts and feelings about this juxtaposition of the supernatural with the ordinary?

How do you feel when someone cooks for you? How do you feel when that person is Jesus?

DAY 3: FEED MY LAMBS

Scripture: John 21:15-19

Imagine you are Peter. What do you make of this conversation?

In your life, who are the sheep and lambs that Jesus might ask you to tend and feed?

DAY 4: GO AND MAKE DISCIPLES

Scripture: Matthew 28:16-20

This is the only account of the disciples meeting the resurrected Jesus in the Gospel of Matthew. Of all the post-resurrection appearances described in the Bible, this one represents the clearest, most forceful commissioning of the disciples to spread the gospel of Jesus Christ. If you are one of these disciples, what do you hear when Jesus speaks of his authority and charges you to make disciples of all nations?

Jesus' words in this passage have been used to justify the effort to Christianize the world. How do *you* interpret them?

What do you hear in Jesus' final words: "I am with you always, to the end of the age"?

DAY 5: PAUL

Scripture: Acts 9:1-19

If you are Paul, what is happening within you at the moment of the flash from heaven, during your three days of blindness, on meeting Ananias?

Have you ever had an experience of "scales falling from your eyes"?

Imagine you are Ananias. What is it like to be told that God has chosen someone you consider your enemy to do God's work? Ananias too had to undergo a conversion. What is that like?

What does this story tell you about God?

DAY 6: PAUL THE MISSIONARY

Scripture: 1 Corinthians 15:3-11

Paul is our only source for this resurrection appearance, which is unique in that it involves hundreds of people. The gospel is spreading, thanks to those who, like Paul, hear and obey the commandment to go to all the world and preach. Imagine you are a member of one of Paul's congregations. What is it about him or his message that moves you?

Paul is acutely aware of his own unfitness to represent Jesus. What makes it possible for him to perform his missionary activity so boldly? What does this say to your own feelings of inadequacy?

DAY 7: REPETITION

Review the last week, rereading your journal entries. Revisit moments of particular grace. How has our concentration on Jesus' commissioning language affected your understanding of or feelings about meeting Jesus after his resurrection?

WEEK 31

ASCENSION AND PENTECOST

This week, the *grace* is:

To fully experience the fire of the Holy Spirit

DAY 1: FORTY DAYS

Scripture: Acts 1:3-5

Imagine being one of the disciples during the 40 days between Jesus' resurrection and ascension. What is that like? What are your expectations? How does your experience with Jesus during this period compare with following Jesus during his pre-Passion ministry? What kinds of things does Jesus teach and preach about during this period?

DAY 2: LOOKING UP

Scripture: Acts 1:6-11

Again, imagine being one of the disciples, witnessing Jesus' ascension. What emotions do you feel? Where is he going? Hear the angels' question, "Why do you stand looking up?" How would you answer this question? Do you have any sense of what comes next?

DAY 3: DESCENT OF THE HOLY SPIRIT

Scripture: Acts 2:1-4

Here the Holy Spirit makes quite an entrance. Pretend you are one of the disciples and make a list of your sensations as the wind sweeps through the room. What do the "tongues as of fire" look like? As a "tongue" rests on you, do you feel changed?

How have you seen/felt/sensed the presence of the Holy Spirit? How does the Holy Spirit make an entrance in your experience?

DAY 4: EACH IN OUR OWN LANGUAGE

Scripture: Acts 2:5-12

We tend to think of "tongue of fire" as a flame, but the word for tongue in the original Greek is also the word used for "language." (It is the root of our modern word "glossary.") The apostles are receiving the gift of language. This gift empowers them to communicate with people all around the known world.

Colloquially, we use the expression, "Now you're speaking my language," meaning that the other person has been able to communicate in a way that you understand. What is your language? What is it like to hear someone speak in your own language? Have you ever had an experience of someone explaining something complex in a manner that you can finally understand?

What gifts of communication do you have?

DAY 5: PETER'S TESTIMONY

Scripture: Acts 2:13-36

This is the first sermon of the Christian church. If you were a Jew in Peter's audience, how would it sound to you?

Nowhere in the Gospels up to now has Peter displayed such eloquence. What has happened to loosen his tongue?

Have you ever listened to a sermon and thought, "I could never do that"? Why?

DAY 6: TEACHING AND FELLOWSHIP, BREAKING OF BREAD AND PRAYERS

Scripture: Acts 2:41-47

"They devoted themselves to the apostles' teaching and fellowship, to the breaking of bread and the prayers." Does this language sound familiar? It is quoted in the Baptismal Covenant in the Book of Common Prayer. Continuing in the apostles' teaching and fellowship, in the breaking of bread and in the prayers is something all baptismal candidates (or their sponsors) vow to do "with God's help."

The next paragraph describes how these early Christians acted out their newfound faith. What strikes you about this description? How does the church as you know it compare?

DAY 7: REPETITION

Review your journal entries for the past week, and for this whole section on Ascension and Pentecost. Revisit moments of particular grace. As we enter the next section, which will address the application of everything we have learned in these exercises, what do you want to take forward with you from this week?

PART VI

INCARNATING

MAKE ME A BLESSING

Ira B. Wilson (1880-1950)

Out in the highways and byways of life, many are weary and sad;
Carry the sunshine where darkness is rife, making the sorrowing glad.
> *Make me a blessing, Make me a blessing, out of my life may*
> *Jesus shine;*
> *Make me a blessing, O Savior, I pray, make me a blessing to*
> *someone today.*

Tell the sweet story of Christ and His love, tell of his power to forgive;
Others will trust Him if only you prove true, every moment you live.
> *Make me a blessing, Make me a blessing, out of my life may*
> *Jesus shine;*
> *Make me a blessing, O Savior, I pray, make me a blessing to*
> *someone today.*

Give as 'twas given to you in your need, love as the Master loved you;
Be to the helpless a helper indeed, unto your mission be true.
> *Make me a blessing, Make me a blessing, out of my life may*
> *Jesus shine;*
> *Make me a blessing, O Savior, I pray, make me a blessing to*
> *someone today.*

Lift Every Voice and Sing: An African American Hymnal (New York: Church Publishing, 1993), 158.

Over the past several weeks, we have followed Jesus closely, trying to know him better that we may follow him more wholeheartedly: literally to become more like him in our own time and place. Just as Jesus was the incarnation of God, we are called to be incarnations of Jesus. Jesus made God visible in human form. We are called to do the same. We are called to incarnate what we have learned about Jesus, about ourselves, about the world, and about ourselves before God.

One of the earmarks of the Ignatian journey is that it is not merely a course of study or a self-improvement project. Ignatius intended his exercises to have a vocational outcome. Even for those not discerning a major life choice like ordination, religious life, or marriage, the exercises are intended to clarify how God is calling you. Never doubt that God is calling you, though that call may be to different things throughout your life. To be baptized means to be called by God.

Completing these exercises naturally suggests the question, "What next?" With what you have learned about yourself and your relationship with Jesus Christ, what will you do now? How will you incarnate Jesus?

This last section is geared to helping you address these questions. The first week of this section is based on a meditation supplied by Ignatius at the end of his exercises, called the Contemplation to Attain the Love of God. The second week offers Ignatian insights into the discernment process, to help you hear and respond lovingly to God's call.

PRAYER EXERCISES

- Dispose yourself for prayer.
- Breathe deeply, at least one cleansing breath.
- Pray for the grace of the week.

- Read through the entire day's prompt before beginning the first step.

- Practice *lectio divina* with the Scripture passages.

- Journal your answers to each day's prayer prompts, or otherwise as you are moved.

- Offer your reflections to God in prayer.

- Do not forget to do your daily examen sometime before bed.

WEEK 32

THE CONTEMPLATION
TO ATTAIN THE LOVE OF GOD

Any discernment is best begun in God's love. Therefore, we begin our discernment of "What next?" with this meditation on God's love.

When Ignatius speaks of attaining the love of God, this does not mean earning God's love. God's love is freely given and therefore cannot be earned. Our goal is to attain the capacity to love as God loves, that our love may grow ever more to resemble God's.

This week, the *grace* is:

An intimate knowledge of my blessings, that filled with gratitude, I may in all things love and serve God.

DAY 1: OBSERVATIONS ABOUT LOVE

Readings:

...Love ought to manifest itself in deeds rather than words. (SE 230)

...Love consists in a mutual sharing of goods... (SE 231)[37]

Scripture: 1 Corinthians 13:4-7

Ignatius begins his Contemplation to Attain the Love of God with the two points cited above. Do you agree with them? Are these observations always true about love? How can human love for God be manifest in deeds? How can love between God and humans be mutual? Are these observations perhaps aspirational rather than always true?

In your journal, list your own observations about love.

---

[37] Ignatius. *Exercises,* 79.

DAY 2: GOD IN ALL

Reading:

> *This is to reflect how God dwells in creatures: in the elements giving them existence, in the plants giving them life, in the animals conferring upon them sensation, in man bestowing understanding. So He dwells in me and gives me being, life, sensation, intelligence; and makes a temple of me, since I am created in the likeness and image of the Divine Majesty.* (SE 235)[38]

Scripture: Psalm 139:7-10

Where do you see God in the created world? Where do you see God in humanity? Where do you see God in yourself? In what ways is the God-in-you related to the God-in-all-creation?

DAY 3: WHAT GOD HAS DONE FOR ME

Reading:

> *I will ponder with great affection how much God our Lord has done for me, and how much He has given me of what He possesses, and finally, how much, as far as He can, the same Lord desires to give Himself to me according to his divine decrees.* (SE 234)[39]

Scripture: Luke 1:46-49

---

[38] Ignatius, *Exercises*, 80.

[39] Ignatius, *Exercises*, 79.

What things, both small and great, has God done for you? Make a list in your journal.

DAY 4: GOD'S LABOR

Reading:

> This is to consider how God works and labors for me in all creatures upon the face of the earth, that is, He conducts Himself as one who labors. Thus, in the heavens, the elements, the plants the fruits, the cattle, etc., He gives being, conserves them, confers life and sensation. (SE 236)[40]

Scripture: Romans 8:26-28

So far this week you have reflected on God's gifts to you. What does it add to your understanding to reflect that God is *constantly* at work in all things on your behalf? How is God at work in your life right now?

DAY 5: GOD THE SOURCE OF ALL BLESSING

Readings:

> This is to consider all blessings and gifts as descending from above. Thus my limited power comes from the supreme and infinite power above, and so too, justice, goodness, mercy, etc., descend from above as the rays of light descend from the sun, and as the waters flow from their fountains. (SE 237)[41]

---

[40] Ignatius, *Exercises*, 80.

[41] Ignatius, *Exercises*, 80.

*All good things around us are sent from heaven above; then thank
the Lord, O thank the Lord, for all his love.*[42]

Scripture: Philippians 4:8-9

Think about all that you regard as good, all that you value, and all
the good that you and others do. Make a list in your journal. Go down the
list, consciously recognizing God as the source of each.

After all this reflection on God's generosity, how do you respond?
Write a letter to God expressing your feelings.

DAY 6: SUSCIPE

Reading:

*Then I will reflect upon myself, and consider, according to all
reason and justice, what I ought to offer the Divine Majesty, that
is, all I possess and myself with it. Thus, as one would do who is
moved by great feeling, I will make this offering of myself:*

*Take, Lord, and receive all my liberty, my memory, my
understanding, and my entire will, all that I have and possess.
Thou hast given all to me. To Thee, O Lord, I return it. All is
Thine, dispose of it wholly according to Thy will. Give me Thy
love and Thy grace, for this is sufficient for me.* (SE 234)[43]

---

[42] Matthias Claudius, *We plow the fields and scatter, The Hymnal 1982* (New York: Church
Publishing, 1985), 291.

[43] Ignatius, *Exercises*, 80.

We have previously considered Ignatius' *Anima Christe* prayer and the Prayer for Generosity (the one that begins "Eternal Lord and King of all") in Week 7 of these exercises. Here is another Ignatian prayer, known as the *Suscipe* (pronounced "soo-she-pay"), which is the Latin word for "receive."

As you have done previously, consider Ignatius' words carefully. Can you imagine being able to pray this prayer from your own heart? If it gives you pause at this point in your life, can you consider the prayer aspirationally?

DAY 7: REPETITION

Review your journal entries for the past week. What has impressed or stuck with you? Revisit any moments of particular grace.

After you have done this, review the Suscipe, and rewrite it in a way that expresses what *you* want to say to God in the way of self-offering.

WEEK 33

VOCATION AND DISCERNMENT

This week, the *grace* is:

To listen in humility for how God may be calling me in love, to hear with joy, and discern with clarity.

DAY 1: PRAYER OF GENEROSITY

Reading: Without reviewing your previous comments on this prayer, reread Ignatius' Prayer of Generosity:

> *Eternal Lord and King of all creation, humbly I come before you. Knowing the support of Mary, your mother, and all your saints, I am moved by your grace to offer myself to you and to your work. I deeply desire to be with you in accepting all wrongs and all abuse and all poverty, both actual and spiritual – and I deliberately choose this, if it is for your greater service and praise. If you, my Lord and King, would so call and choose me, then take and receive me into such a way of life.* (SE 98)[44]

Again, without turning back in your journal to review your previous comments, write about how you feel about them now that you have completed these many weeks of study, prayer, and reflection.

Now, go back and read your first journal entry about the Prayer for Generosity for Week 7, Day 3. How does what you have written today compare? What evolution do you perceive in your thoughts, feelings, and prayer about accepting whatever may befall you in serving and praising God?

---

[44] Fleming, *Exercises*, 67.

DAYS 2 AND 3: COMPREHENSIVE REPETITION

Reading: Your journal, especially your repetitions

What movement do you perceive in yourself over the many weeks of this journey? Which section, reading, or prayer prompt did you like the best? Which section seemed to elicit the most growth in you? How have these exercises changed you?

Have a colloquy with Jesus, the Father, the Holy Spirit, or Mother Mary about your journey so far. Listen to how they reply to you.

DAY 4: YOUR GIFTS

Scripture: Romans 12:4-8; 1 Corinthians 12:4-11; Ephesians 4:1-7

What do you see as your special gifts? St. Paul lists many spiritual gifts, but his lists are not exhaustive. Have you a gift that he does not list?

Our gifts are the best indication of where God is calling us. How are you using your gifts to God's service?

What other ways might there be of using your gifts to serve and praise God?

DAY 5: JOY AND PASSION

Reading:

The place God calls you to is the place where your deep gladness and the world's deep hunger meet.

~Frederick Buechner[45]

---

[45] Frederick Buechner, *Wishful Thinking* (New York: Collins, 1973), 13.

The notion that doing the godly thing is always hard is a fallacy. Often joy at doing something is an indication not only of God's gift to you, but also of where God is calling you. What activity gives you the greatest joy? How might you expand your exercise of that activity to serve and praise God?

Alternatively, what issues excite you the most? Where do you feel the greatest energy? The passion you feel about certain subjects is also an indicator of where God might be calling you.

Taking into consideration your movement through these exercises, your understanding of your gifts, and where you find joy and passion, how might God be calling you? Is there a new ministry to which you might be called? Are you perhaps being called to go deeper into prayer? Or are you simply being called to continue to wait on the Lord?

In your journal, complete this sentence: At this time and place, I believe God may be calling me to_____.

You don't have to be absolutely sure about your call at this point. Tomorrow, we will consider the Ignatian method of testing a perceived call in a section he calls "Making a Good and Correct Choice of a Way of Life."

DAY 6: DISCERNMENT

Reading:

This is to place before my mind the object with regard to which I wish to make a choice...

It is necessary to keep as my aim the end for which I am created, that is, the praise of God our Lord and the salvation of my soul. Besides this, I must be indifferent, without any inordinate attachment.... I should be like a balance at equilibrium, without leaning to either side, that I might be ready to follow whatever I perceive is more for the glory and praise of God our Lord and for the salvation of my soul.

I should beg God our Lord to deign to move my will, and to bring to my mind what I ought to do in this matter that would be more for his praise and glory. Then I should use the understanding to weigh the matter with care and fidelity, and make my choice in conformity with what would be more pleasing to His most holy will.

This will be to weigh the matter by reckoning the ... advantages and benefits [of my choice] as well as the disadvantages and danger.

After I have gone over and pondered in this way every aspect of the matter in question, I will consider which alternative appears more reasonable. Then I must come to a decision in the matter under deliberation because of weightier motives presented to my reason, and not because of any sensual inclination.

After such a choice or decision, the one who has made it must turn with great diligence to prayer in the presence of God our Lord, and offer Him his choice that the Diving Majesty may deign to accept and confirm if it is for His greater service and praise. (SE 178-183)[46]

---

[46] Ignatius, *Exercises*, 58-59.

To summarize, this process has six steps:

1. Identify the decision you intend to make. (It's easiest if you define one alternative in positive form, such as: "I will run for vestry.")

2. Remembering that the ultimate aim is to serve and praise God, cultivate an open mind (without attachments).

3. Ask God's inspiration and guidance.

4. Weigh advantages and disadvantages.

5. Make a provisional decision.

6. Ask God to confirm it, and be alert for signs of this confirmation.

If you identified a course of action yesterday, subject it to this method. What do you conclude? In your journal, complete this sentence: In order to serve and praise God, I am going to: _____.

As you might imagine, this method of discernment is adaptable to almost any decision you may face. You may wish to save this article for future reference.

DAY 7: REPETITION

Review the last week, rereading your journal entries. What was easy, and what was hard? Where has God been in your ruminations?

Have one last colloquy with Jesus, the Father, the Holy Spirit, or Mother Mary in which you share about your experience during these exercises. Record any last words in your journal.

BENEDICTION AND FAREWELL

It is an exceedingly odd thing to be an author: to be connected in some small way to people you will probably never know. If you have made it this far into the book, you and I have shared much. I thank you for the investment you have made in this project, and I pray with all my heart that, through it, God has blessed you.

After an intense shared experience, it is difficult to know how to say goodbye, but the best way is "goodbye" in its original sense: "God be with you." So, dear fellow travelers, God be with you. I leave you with my favorite benediction, a condensation of Isaiah 42, verses 1 and 4:

> *Thus says the Lord:*
> *You are mine, and I made you.*
> *You are precious to me, and I love you.*

The blessing of God, Father, Son and Holy Spirit, be amongst you and remain with you always.

Amen.

Rockingham, Virginia

Advent, 2021

BIBLIOGRAPHY

Buechner, Frederick. *Wishful Thinking*. New York: Collins, 1973.

Bourgeault, Cynthia. *Centering Prayer and Inner Awakening*. Cambridge: Cowley, 2004.

Claudius, Matthias. "We Plow the Fields and Scatter." *The Hymnal 1982*. New York: Church Publishing, 1985.

Cummings, E. E. "i thank You God for most this amazing." *Complete Poems, 1904-1962 by E. E. Cummings*, edited by George J. Firmage. New York: Liveright, 1979.

Dyckman, Katherine, Mary Garvin, and Elizabeth Liebert. *The Spiritual Exercises Reclaimed: Uncovering Liberating Possibilities for Women*. New York: Paulist, 2001.

"Find a Spiritual Director/Companion Guide." Spiritual Directors International, last modified 2021, https://www.sdicompanions.org/find-a-spiritual-director-companion/ (downloaded 8/11/21).

Fleming, David L. *The Spiritual Exercises of Saint Ignatius: A Literal Translation & A Contemporary Reading*. Chestnut Hill, MA: Institute of Jesuit Sources, 1991.

Fox, Matthew. *Christian Mystics: 365 Readings and Meditations*. Novato, CA: New World Library, 2011.

Hymnal 1982, ver. "Stabat Mater." *The Hymnal 1982*. New York: Church Hymnal.

Ignatius of Loyola. *The Spiritual Exercises of St. Ignatius: Based on Studies in the Language of the Autograph*, translated by Louis J. Puhl, S.J. New York: Vintage, 2000.

Johnson, James Weldon. "The Creation," *God's Trombones: Seven Negro Sermons in Verse*. New York: Penguin Classics, 2008.

Julian of Norwich. *Revelations of Divine Love*. Digireads.com, 2020. Kindle.

Keating, Thomas. *Open Mind, Open Heart*. New York: Bloomsbury, 2019.

McCullen, Susan. "You Can Relax Now." susanmccullen.com.

Merrill, Nan C. *Psalms for Praying: An Invitation to Wholeness*. New York: Continuum, 2007.

Merton, Thomas. "The Merton Prayer." *Thoughts in Solitude* Copyright © 1956, 1958 by The Abbey of Our Lady of Gethsemani. (downloaded from https://reflections.yale.edu/article/seize-day-vocation-calling-work/merton-prayer, October 20, 2021.)

Noll, Shaina. "You Can Relax Now." *Songs for the Inner Child*. Singing Heart, 2003.

Walford, William. "Sweet Hour of Prayer." *Lift Every Voice and Sing II: An African American Hymnal.* New York: Church Publishing, 1993.

Wilson, Ira B. "Make me a Blessing." *Lift Every Voice and Sing II: An African American Hymnal.* New York: Church Publishing, 1993.